The
Twentysomething
Guide to
Creative
Self-Employment

The
Twentysomething Guide to Creative Self-Employment

Making Money While Keeping Your Freedom

Jeff Porten

PRIMA PUBLISHING

PRIMA PUBLISHING and colophon are trademarks of Prima Communications, Inc.

Library of Congress Cataloging-in-Publication Data

Porten, Jeff.
  The twentysomething guide to creative self-employment : making money while keeping your freedom / by Jeff Porten.
    p.   cm.
  Includes index.
  ISBN 0-7615-0445-1
  1. Self-employed—Handbooks, manuals, etc.   2. New business enterprises—Management—Handbooks, manuals, etc.   3. Small business—Management—Handbooks, manuals, etc.   4. Entrepreneurship—Handbooks, manuals, etc.   I. Title.
HD8036.P67   1996
658'.041—dc20   96-611
                                                                       CIP

96 97 98 99 00 01 AA 10 9 8 7 6 5 4 3 2 1
Printed in the United States of America

How to Order:

Single copies may be ordered from Prima Publishing, P.O. Box 1260BK, Rocklin, CA 95677; telephone (916) 632-4400. Quantity discounts are also available. On your letterhead, include information concerning the intended use of the books and the number of books you wish to purchase.

*This book is dedicated to the memory of
Bettina Pruckmayr, who should have been
able to attend my first book party.
We miss you.*

CONTENTS

ACKNOWLEDGMENTS

*M*y life and this book owe a lot to a number of people, without whom both would be far more dreary. First up are my parents, David and Lois Porten. It's common to thank Mom and Dad in this section, and as you'll read in the book, they had a lot to do with my survival during the early days of my business. Thanks, folks.

My girlfriend, Heather Hamilton, has put up with the best and worst moods that my business and book have inflicted on me. My personality is a pain to begin with, and she's qualified for sainthood for putting up with it and taking care of me when I needed it. I'd say more, but she'd rip my head off if I expounded in print.

A fair number of people have helped me out along the way. Thanks to Shari Bart, John Bertland, Mike Blaine, Joseph Friedman, Matt Han, Daniel Helfman, Jeffrey Itell, Barry Lebowitz, Hilary Locker (who got me thinking like an author in the first place), Marc Paul, Ken Ray, Leslie Soforenko, Dirk Trojan, Steve Walsh, and Michael Weinmayr. Apologies to anyone I missed.

My editors at Prima, Greg Aaron and Lisa Armstrong, have been patient and very helpful dealing with a first time author. It's been as painless as possible and I thank them for that.

Saved for last, my agent, Robert Shepard, is owed a great deal of the credit for this book's existence. His professional services have been far above and beyond the call of duty, and his witty advice and friendship have been rocks of Gibraltar for me since the day we met. Thanks for everything.

The
Twentysomething Guide to Creative Self-Employment

CHAPTER 1

Out of the Rat Race

Ours is the first generation in the history of our culture in which most people think their own lives will not be better than their parents' lives. The changing economy and the scarcity of good paying jobs have left many of us in a constant state of low level fear, uncertainty, and doubt.

Sure, you've got a lot going for you. You're in the prime of your life. You're educated. You're credentialed with a high school or college diploma. You've got a couple of years of full-time or part-time work experience under your belt. You've got a range of skills you can call your own—even if not all of them are necessarily the kind that puts food on the table. You might even have a good job with a salary, benefits, and a 401(k) plan.

And you're restless. Welcome to occupation angst, 1990s style, the world where good people go years without getting a job, or settle for one way beneath their skills—and, more importantly, way beneath their dreams—where high hopes and big plans collide head on in what more jaded, more experienced friends and mentors call the Real World.

You might be anywhere in the long chain of events that leads to the demoralizing, deadening conclusion that your life might not turn out the way you had planned. Some people hit it in college, junior year or thereabouts, when graduation is far off yet still a nagging concern, like an execution date set by a state with long appeals. Others get it a little later, senior year, when the job search starts full swing and the résumé needs to be as polished as the shoes, with the scuff marks on both hidden as well as possible. Maybe it sinks in a hell of a lot deeper when it's three months past graduation and the hunt is still on.

And the job itself? Nirvana for a few, drudge work for the masses. Ask a hundred recent grads if they find their work fulfilling, challenging, financially rewarding, and energizing enough to have them springing out of bed each morning with a twinkle in their eye. What response will you get? Depends on how many honest people you know—but probe a little into those seemingly honest "yes" replies and see how many people are happy now thanks to the expectations of rewards later, after they've made manager, gotten that promotion or bonus, or simply paid their dues.

Wherever you go, same story: internships that pay nothing because that's what the market will bear, twentysomethings holding down two or even three jobs to cover bills, fierce competition for plum jobs (and even those might look like prunes from the inside), and, in general, resignation that this is the way things are.

Hey, that's why shows and movies like *Friends* and *Reality Bites* are so popular among our set. Our role models are Jennifer Aniston busing tables and Janeane Garofalo folding sweaters at The Gap, or Ben Stiller living the corporate lifestyle and fundamentally missing the point, and we say,

"Yeah, that's the way these things go." Maybe corporate drudgery outranks grunt work in the Great Hierarchy of Entry Level Work, but that doesn't make it any more captivating. Just easier to rationalize.

It doesn't have to be that way.

My Ticket Out—
Perhaps Yours Too

For me, it was around 1989 when I started thinking, "There's gotta be a better way." It was my junior year in college, and graduation was looking like Scylla and Charybdis combined, no way out and no way through. So long, extracurricular activities (which always outranked academics in my book). Fare thee well, campus. Dining Services, I hardly knew ye. Ciao social life, friends, my comfortable niche.

So when D day finally rolled around and the tassel flipped to the left side, I got a card from my parents that read, "Congratulations, graduate! With *that* degree you expect to get a job?" Great kidders, my parents. But there was a grain of truth to it, since I had to admit the classified listings went straight from Accounting to Auto Repair, unceremoniously skipping over American Civilization, which was my personal liberal arts, no clear job major.

Faced with impending doom, I resolutely squared my shoulders, steeled my will, and girded my loins. Then I fled screaming back to graduate school, the Last Refuge of the Overcompetent. At the same university, no less.

That two year master's stretched out to a three year master's. Flash forward to 1992. I was now starting year seven of college, if you're still counting—Lord knows my friends and parents were. My fraternity nicknamed me Jeffus Eternitus. And I was realizing that all I'd really done was delay the inevitable.

Now don't get me wrong. Grad school was great; I learned a lot, did a lot of cool things, and traveled to a bunch of exotic places. (Best of all, tuition was a free ride thanks to one of my mother's employee perks. Thanks, Mom.) But September 1992 didn't find me any more prepared to deal with leaving school than September 1989 had—in the sense that I had no clear idea what it was I wanted to do.

However, after seven years I was pretty damn certain what I *didn't* want to do. Chief among them was spend an eighth year on campus. I had clearly overstayed my welcome and gotten all I could out of that phase of my life.

I couldn't see myself going the corporate route. That was fine for my business school friends—after all, that was what they had trained for. They saw their comfy salaries (already approaching six figures, in some cases), benefits packages, and corporate advancement ladders and said, "Sign me up!" That didn't sit right with me—because I had seen too clearly what they had given up: their hobbies, outside interests, and political involvements.

I also didn't want to give up certain aspects of my lifestyle that I felt were important to my character. I'm a night owl— if it weren't for 2 A.M., this book never would have been written. Those few times when I've experimented with a nine to five workday, it's always turned out to be a bad idea. I could pull it off responsibly for a short time, but it was just that, something I pulled off—not something I wanted to make a habit of, and definitely not a modus operandi for my life.

Worse still are the consequences of that kind of life. You wake up one morning, and it's Monday, the fiftieth or one hundredth or two hundredth Monday since you started, and you're wondering just where the hell all that time went.

Those are the main things that did it for me—but maybe other aspects of the corporate lifestyle irk you more: the boss whose dictates and goals will always take precedence over yours, or the numbing certainty that you just *might* get a five percent raise six months from now, or that promotion, if you're lucky, and there's not a damn thing you can do about it if your boss decides otherwise. Or perhaps you're most disturbed by the vagaries of office politics and culture, where you'll have to deal with competitive coworkers, possible sexual harassment, and committee meetings and incompetence ad infinitum.

Face it, even in the best workplaces, this kind of work life is your basic Industrial Revolution McJob. Some people thrive in this kind of environment. Others successfully adapt. Many unsuccessfully adapt, making an income, but not really making a life.

I don't know which kind of worker I am. I blew all that off entirely, and took the entrepreneurial route. I became my own boss on Day One, in a brand new city, and struck out for fame and fortune all on my own.

It was scary as hell. Three years later, it still causes some truly terrifying moments. But I can't understand why more people don't do this—especially people our age, when our commitments are fewer, our needs are simpler, and we're biologically at the best time of our lives to pull the occasional all-nighter or put in the insane workweek when the need arises. And it will.

The biggest selling point for me, though, can be summarized as follows: "Why the hell not? If it doesn't work out, I'll look for a job *then*. But I'll do this *now*."

It was the best decision I ever made. I don't know anyone who's got a better job than me—and trust me, I know a lot of people. You can't beat it in terms of quality of life. Sure, there are times when the stress gets so bad that I wish I had some elephant tranquilizers handy. But most sunny afternoons I'm out for a walk in the park, or sipping a coffee at my favorite sidewalk café. I wake up most mornings around nine or ten, and make most of my business calls in my bathrobe—don't tell my clients. Suits and ties are only for face-to-face meetings, which are usually two or three times a week.

There are trade-offs, naturally. I can take a day off whenever I please, but in return I usually do at least some work most weekends and holidays. I actually resent holidays, because they're usually perfectly good weekdays when I'm at my desk but my prospects aren't at theirs, so there's zero chance of new checks arriving.

The reward is total personal freedom. Like John Philpot Curran (1750–1817) said, "Eternal vigilance is the price of liberty"—which in this context translates to a lot of responsibility for keeping your customers and clients happy. But it's totally on your terms. It's not in the least bit easy, but it can be exhilarating.

Knowing a Fortune When You Find One

Entrepreneurship is all about making your fortune—setting goals and working daily to accomplish them. It's not about making *a* fortune, although a bunch of self-employed people have managed to do just that. If you want to become self-employed to get rich, more power to you—it's a risky venture, but wealth is one of the potential payoffs.

More important, though, is making your own fortune, in the sense of being fortunate rather than making money. Making your fortune means enjoying your work. It means not wondering where the hell you're going, or what you've been doing with your life recently. It means taking charge of those things that are truly important to you and making time for them in your life. It's the best possible way of building a life while you build a career, and entwining your values and needs into the short-term and long-term goals of both.

It means, ultimately, looking around you once in a while and feeling damned lucky to be who you are and where you are, even though luck—in the capricious sense—has nothing to do with it. Luck is something you make with hard work and effort. It's being in the right place at the right time—by being in many places at many times until the right one hits.

You make your fortune by building your life, piece by piece, in the time and manner of your choosing—not as a part-time hobby squeezed in around a nine to five McJob, but as an ongoing, real part of your day-to-day work and personal goals. Entrepreneurship is the only way I know to ascertain that you'll spend your life as you see fit, and not as others would have you spend it. It's the only way to enjoy the fruits of your labor, rather than have them skimmed off by employers and coworkers. It's the only way to truly determine what you're worth and whether your ambitions can be reached on your terms.

Entrepreneurship gives you the opportunity to create the guidelines for success and failure, and to set your own rules for the game.

Deciding to Take Control

As you may have guessed, I'm gung ho about self-employment. I'll assume that you are too, or you're thinking about it, if you've gotten this far.

It's not a decision to be taken lightly. Total freedom means total control, and with that goes the complete ability to really screw up your life. If you're not sure where you're going or why you're getting into this, it's a cinch to wander in circles and get nowhere. No one is going to help you out there unless you find mentors and colleagues, and that part of the job is entirely up to you.

Being on your own is scary and difficult. It has some of the greatest rewards that a career can offer. But the chances for failure are real, large, and usually imminent. This book will help you navigate those shoals to some extent, but ultimately you're on your own.

If you think you can handle all that, then let's get to work. Here's some of what we'll cover:

- Finding your bliss, talents, and skills—in that order—and what to do if you're not sure you have any
- The basics of how to do the business thing: income, cash flow, taxes, legalities, and other distractions
- The niceties of striking out on your own: business cards, marketing, clothing, and other ways of not appearing unemployed
- Networking and finding customers and clients—the people who keep you from being unemployed
- Keeping yourself sane and well fed when you don't have any business (difficult, at best) and when you do (even harder)
- Finding help—books, resources, and computer stuff; the things I've found indispensable and what I could have done without

What you'll be getting here are the best ideas and worst mistakes I've made in the last few years, and some straight advice on how best to deal with them. I can't tell you how to become a millionaire, and this is certainly no get rich quick guide. But I can tell you how to build a satisfying life for yourself, one where you won't wonder why you're dragging yourself out of bed in the morning, or feel like you're handing over your life for little in return. You'll be the master of your fate, the captain of your soul—or at least as close as you can get in this lifetime.

The first question is whether you're up for the job.

CHAPTER 2

Don't "Just Do It!"

"*J*ust do it!" That's the supposed maxim of our generation, right? Thanks to a few sneaker and soda companies, we're the ones who are supposed to go off half-cocked, recklessly embracing new experiences and new adventures—and, of course, breaking out into a fashionable sweat.

That might be the right way to psych yourself up for skydiving in Rollerblades, but I don't recommend it for starting a business. Both involve hurtling at high speeds, heart-racing excitement, and the promise of a heavy impact without knowing if you'll be able to stand up when you land. Starting a business is a lot more likely to hurt.

That's not too surprising, when you think about it, since just about everyone who skydives knows to check the 'chute, oil the skates, and make sure that all the things that life depends on are in fine working order. But many folks who go off into business don't make such a careful inventory of their own equipment, including their talents, desires, will to succeed, and self-destructive habits that might get in the way. That kills them as surely as pancaking into a cornfield from 10,000 feet—and it does it slowly, unglamorously, by breaking down their spirits.

As wonderful and self-fulfilling as entrepreneurship can be, it is absolutely not everyone's cup of joe. Your first question must be, is this really what I want to do? More important might be the question, is this what I need—what I'm *driven*—to do?

There are many comfortable, middle-aged people who dream daily of telling their bosses to kiss off and walking out of their safe corporate lifestyles to make their fortune—and never do. For most of them, the fantasy of being self-employed is its own reward, a chance to blow off some mental steam, and they won't ever go off on their own because they secretly, unconsciously, prefer to just dream about it.

Then there's the small minority who remain trapped in their jobs, yearning to strike out on their own but unable to take that step, fenced in by their own fears. They worry that those luxuries that have insidiously turned themselves into vital needs—the large apartment, the nice car, the evening decaf latte with biscotti that costs more than lunch—will disappear if they leave the safety of corporate life.

Fortunately, our generation is the least susceptible to being wedded to our material goods—not because we're special, but because we're least likely to have set our material needs in stone. A twentysomething genuinely needs her Miata a hell of a lot less than a thirtysomething with kids needs his Volvo.

If you've picked up this book because you're well-paid but unfulfilled in your work, take a look at all your stuff and ask yourself if there's anything you own, or an expensive routine you maintain, that makes up for the hollow space in your soul that gets a little larger every day you spend in useless meetings, every hour you commute in traffic to work, every time a lower life-form in upper management tells you what to do and how to do it in excruciating detail.

If material things make up for all that, then be honest with yourself. There's nothing wrong with needing a few luxuries—I know people who would give up their apartments and become homeless if they could wire up their sewer grates for ESPN. But you have to know which of those luxuries have really become essentials for you—and make damn sure they're fully paid for before you do anything as risky as going solo.

If you're coming from the other direction, like I did, fresh out of college and with nothing to lose, you're still not quite out of the woods. College for most of us was Fantasyland without the monorail. It's very easy to get used to that free and easy lifestyle, with no real responsibilities, no one to answer to—and no bills to pay. There are ways to play a similar game after college, but you'll be much better off with those tactics in a faceless organization than out on your own.

I learned that when I moved to Washington, D.C., and my landlord laid it on the line for me. Rent was due on the fifth. If it was one day late, I owed him twenty bucks more. If it was six days late, he'd file an honest-to-God lawsuit against me for nonpayment of rent, and I'd owe him every penny of the court costs. No extensions, no dog-ate-my-paycheck excuses. I realized he meant it when I went in to negotiate an easy-payment plan one October, and he said, "We get it all by Friday or you're in court." So Mom FedEx'ed a check that month (and a few months after that). Nowadays I pay my own rent, and thanks to those early experiences, there's always a small but significant pleasure in that mundane monthly event.

When you work for yourself, there won't be much room for excuses or gamesmanship. When you can't pay the rent, you can't blame a stingy boss who doesn't pay you what you're worth, because you'll literally be making exactly what you're worth.

If you do it right, I guarantee you'll be worth very little at first but will eventually make a minimum wage and then a comfortable one, and then maybe even a generous one. Wealthy beyond your dreams is also an option if you have a real winner of an idea—but don't count on it right away. What you can count on is the constant, never-ending, nagging fear of failure, nipping at your heels if you stop to rest for too long. Sometimes, however, that very fear will motivate you.

What does *that* mean? It means that my rent is paid this month, and I've got money in checking for the next, but the month after that is still wide open. If in the next six weeks all of my clients decided to install aluminum siding on their aquariums instead of giving me some business, then I'd either have to dip into my sometimes-nonexistent savings, or Mom might have to send me another rent check. That's not just debt, that's humiliation. Of course, similar pain is there for the salary types, as well, if their jobs hit the chopping block, but the illusion of permanence helps to ward off the cold sweats for them. We're not so lucky.

So why live with this kind of misery? You can go to the library and check out every book on entrepreneurship, ask any self-employed person you like, and you'll find that it often boils down to one word: freedom. The freedom to make your own decisions, to set your own salary and schedule, and to revise and change and constantly pursue your own goals.

And, of course, the freedom to have that second cup of coffee in the morning and field your first phone calls while you're still in your bathrobe. I put a high value on having that kind of control over my time, which no sane boss would ever allow. It also means that I've had almost no vacation days this past year, including weekends and holidays—if you define vacation as "a day in which no work is done and the computer is left turned off"—but I've logged about 50,000 miles of travel to various cities, states, countries, and continents, pretty much whenever I pleased. I don't get paid for sick days or vacation, but I don't have to count them either—and I don't need a silly excuse when I feel like sleeping in.

Those are some of my reasons for doing what I'm doing. You might have different ones—and don't kid yourself into thinking that you'll get to sleep late if your entrepreneurial venture includes full-time employees or a storefront operation. You have to make sure that the rewards of your particular choice match what you need to get out of it, or it's going to burn you out fast.

Can You Hack It?

Most entrepreneurial books and courses start with one of those cute questionnaires where you fill in the blanks with option a, b, or c, and at the end out pops a numerical rating indicating your suitability for being on your own. I'm not going to inflict one of those on you, mainly because the dozen times I did it myself I somehow always got exactly the answer I was looking for. Besides, we're talking about a life-changing, stupendous decision here; it's not the kind of thing you boil down to a *Cosmo* poll.

If you're considering taking the plunge, the main question on your mind has to be, can I hack it? I'm deliberately using the colloquial term here, because it is up to you what "hacking it" means. It could mean being wildly successful financially. It could mean supporting yourself frugally while you figure out what your next stage will be. It could mean lowering your stress level, or rocketing into a fast-lane, jet-set, cellular-phone lifestyle. But it should definitely mean having your inner needs met and yourself expressed in the work you do, the energy you invest, and the time you spend.

Hacking it is whatever you make it out to be. You probably already have an unconscious knowledge of what you consider it to be, and are also fairly certain that whatever you're doing now doesn't quite cut it—or you wouldn't be wasting your time thinking about it. When your job doesn't feel right on a really deep level, or the career path you've planned (or had chosen for you) has you staring at the ceiling at 4 A.M., you can be pretty sure you're not hacking it now.

When that happens, you can almost feel your spark fading away. Loss of faith in yourself is one of the worst possible outcomes of any venture, and it's a special tragedy when it happens to someone our age. If there's an overriding reason for my proselytizing, it's because too many jobs suck the lifeblood out of us, at precisely the time when the world should be our own personal oyster.

Self-employment is not without its pitfalls, including the risk of spiritual destruction. But the best way to avoid that is to understand as best as possible your own needs, desires, and motives. And the only way to do that is to write it down. You have to set down, concretely, where you are at this stage in your life, and why you're considering this step.

Our First, Last, and Only Writing Exercise

Well, not really—later, when we talk about business plans, it'll be a good idea to jot down a few things. But some folks recommend that you write so many essays in preparation for self-employment that you'll think you're applying to college again.

All I want you to do is really think about who you are, where you are, and where you're going. Here's how I recommend you do it: sketch out your future following these four possible scenarios.

Path of Least Resistance. Where will you be in the next three years if you continue along the same route you're taking now, with no extraordinary steps along the way? Will the time spent be fulfilling to you? Will the end result (as if any life process has one) meet your standards of success? Will your sense of satisfaction grow or lessen?

Hacking It. If you do set off on your own, what will you need to get by over the next three years? Think of minimum financial requirements to keep body and soul together (or apart, if you prefer). Consider what you would need to have a desirable lifestyle, stress level, personal time, and social life, and explore what those would be in specific terms. When you're hacking it, you're living a life of simple decency, general contentment, and sometimes even happiness—but what does that mean to you? Be honest with yourself about what your family, friends, and peers would think, what you would need to impress or mollify them, and how important that is to you.

Success. What would you need to consider yourself really successful in three years? Would that be best expressed in financial terms, or by some other method? What would success mean to you in terms of your friendships, family relations, romantic life, and inner self? (Leave off that last bit if it feels too New Age for you.) Again, who do you need to impress, and how important is that? Now reread what you've written: is success for you a destination, a goalpost, or the process itself?

The Abyss. Now, the hard part. What is abject, utter, total failure to you? What happens when you have no sales or clients, your savings are spent, your credit cards maxed, and Emilio Estevez shows up to repo your car? What would the worst possible outcome be if your venture blew up? What would you have left to draw upon? What would remain constant in your life, regardless of failure? What would you do next?

If you're reading this book the same way I read *The Seven Habits of Highly Effective People* a couple of years ago, when you got to the above list, you read each paragraph, stared out into space for a minute or two, thought about it, and went on to the next one. I'm recommending that you actually stop, put this book down, and write down your thoughts. You're not setting your life in stone here—what you are doing is recording your thoughts, hopes, and dreams at this moment for your own benefit later on, so you can see where you've gone and how you've changed. As we'll see, entrepreneurship can be a frighteningly vague process, and the more you've written down, the more grounded you'll feel.

Another valuable exercise is to change the time period from three years to one year, six months, or even ten years. Personally, I can visualize myself in ten years about as easily as I can visualize myself dead—which is to say, not at all. But it's worth knowing lifetime goals, and short-term goals, and seeing if you can find a coherent trend leading from the short-term to mid-term to lifetime.

All right, so now you've got an idea of four possible futures. Here's where you try to bare your soul and decide whether this is a risk worth taking.

First, visualize as clearly as possible your path of least resistance. Is that tolerable to you? Abhorrent? Not as bad as it might have seemed? Since this path will be firmly within your comfort zone, you'll need a strong push (or an equally strong pull from a better alternative) to break you out of this line.

Second, picture yourself hacking it. Remember, this is the one that's pretty much contentment, if not quite oneness with the Godhead. How attractive is this picture to you? What does hacking it provide that you might not be getting out of your present life? Is hacking it good enough, even if you never become "successful" as you've defined it?

Third, see yourself successful. Taste it, smell it, grasp it, fantasize it every which way you can—and remember that depending on how you've defined it, you may not ever quite get there. Or you may be there on Day One of the new business. How does it feel? How much does it draw you in? Does it inspire you—*compel you*—to pursue your own business?

Fourth . . . you guessed it. Think about rock bottom. Really put yourself there, until you can feel failure in the pit of your stomach like a ball of ice the size of a twenty-pound Perdue roaster. If you're doing this part right, you'll literally be able to taste it in your mouth. (Failure, that is, not chicken.)

Well? How bad is it? Do not forget for a minute that failure is always a possibility, no matter how good you are or how ironclad your business ideas. I don't care if you're selling bulletproof vests to the Crips—something can always go wrong and make your perfect idea go sour.

Does the lure of success outweigh the possibility of failure? More importantly, will hacking it fulfill you enough to make this worthwhile? If you can build the lifestyle you want in the pursuit of your definition of success, and make the journey itself fulfilling and rewarding, then not only will the sting of failure be lessened, but the probability of it ever occurring will drop. If your work is fulfilling in and of itself, then of course you'll work harder, better, and increase your chances of success.

When I started out, my own personal twenty-pound frozen bird was the thought that I might have to close up shop in Washington and move back to my parents' house in Philadelphia with my tail between my legs, and with all my friends knowing that I hadn't lived up to my expectations, or to how I had mouthed off to them. I never had to seriously consider moving home, but the thought of it scared the hell out of me.

The nice thing about cold fear in the gut, though, is that it tends to warm your fires in the morning. Some people become successful because they pursue their goals, others because they flee their fears. The healthiest method is probably heavy on the former with a dose of the latter. Fear can paralyze you, or it can spur you on—but you have to live with it, because it rarely goes away.

I'm comfortably hacking it right now, thanks in large part to a list of steady clients, writing this book, rewarding relationships with my family, friends, and girlfriend, and a spiffy new apartment that is luxurious compared with where I was a few months ago. But I wouldn't call myself successful, not just yet—and that's because I didn't set my goals in writing a year ago. If you had asked me then, hypothetically, if where I am now was "success," I would have said yes without a second thought. But now that I'm here, the bar has been set a few meters higher. That's the price of ambition: never being satisfied

R ule of thumb: don't mouth off—you've got enough to live up to already.

with where you are. Setting goals in writing is the best way I know of to nail down your dreams. You can always continue to dream bigger and better things, but don't forget to recognize when you've lived up to your old dreams, and to take that opportunity to wallow in self-satisfaction for a little while.

I don't know if I'll ever look at myself and think, "Wow, I'm really successful." There will always be the next hurdle to clear, and I'm the type who looks more to the hurdles ahead than to the road behind. If I weren't aware of this fact, in a few years I could be in the same exact situation I'm in now, but totally depressed about not being successful. Know yourself well, or you'll find yourself in the same shoes.

Half-Assed Efforts and Complete Asses

So now you know what hacking it means to you. Next question: can you do it?

According to some estimates, about four out of every five businesses go bust within their first five years. There's some commotion about that statistic, since it counts as a business failure if Bill Gates hires you for a half-mil in three years. Regardless, it's clear across the board that more businesses fail than succeed.

There are many reasons why businesses go bust. Most of them boil down to finances—too much money going out, not enough coming in, until one day a large man named Bruno shows up at the door to repossess your face. That's what you get for getting your start-up funds from Corleone Savings and Loan.

But behind financial issues lie the real reasons why businesses go bad. They include bad luck, bad accounting, bad hiring, poor location, poor health, and inadequate planning. All of these factors can be controlled to some extent or another—*especially* luck, which I believe you make for yourself. More on that later.

The biggest causes of business failures, though, based on my unscientific observations, are lack of passion, inadequacy of commitment, and failure to strive. I sum these up under the umbrella term of "half-assed effort." A half-assed effort is the quick road to total failure, and making a complete ass of yourself.

If you'll pardon the pun, you can seriously work your butt off and still be doing a half-assed effort. Likewise, putting in a hundred percent doesn't have to mean putting in a hundred hours a week. It means doing what you do extremely well, and choosing what you do even better.

Unfortunately, the difference between one and the other is often a matter of experience, and it's not always possible to really know how you're doing. It turned out that I was seriously half-assed the first year of my own business, but I didn't know it until I had the benefit of hindsight in year two. I was lucky enough to make it through that—but with slightly less generous parents or a slightly less pigheaded attitude, I'd be working at Megalith Conglomerate Incorporated today. I don't know if you're in a position to be that lucky, so here's how to avoid a half-assed effort.

Rule One: Don't Be Self-Employed As Your Last Alternative to Being Unemployed. A lot of folks start working for themselves because no one else wants them—for the time being, anyway. Or they think self-employment is a great way to pad a résumé so they don't have to say they spent nine months watching Joey Buchanan on *One Life to Live.*

Now, the weird part of this is that those are two damn good reasons to start self-employment. You'll learn a lot, you'll develop some new skills, you'll get off your butt, and you might even be successful enough to tell a recruiter to take a flying leap when he calls you back in six months. It's OK if the road to self-employment is paved with desperation—*but you can't act like it is!* People who do that aren't entrepreneurs, they're just self-unemployed. Call them untrepreneurs.

Picture this: after four or five months of unemployment, Joe gets a job. He shows up for work on Monday at around eleven. He's wearing sweats, he hasn't shaven, and he walks in eating Corn Pops straight from the box with a chocolate milk chaser. When his boss asks him what's up, he tells her that he's been on a sloppy schedule for a while, and it's going to take him about three months to make the transition back to a job—but don't worry, by March he'll be back to pressed suits and clean shaves.

Sounds ludicrous, right? But that's how untrepreneurs make the transition to self-employment. They'll think about it for a while, then ponder it, then write down a few things, and then they'll see if they can fit it in between job interviews, résumé rewrites, and Joey Buchanan. Maybe six months later, if they still haven't found a job, their entrepreneurial work will expand to where it's a full-time sort of thing. At that point some people chuck the job search and really make a go of the business—but the untrepreneur will put in the time without putting in the spirit.

Untrepreneurs haven't gotten their business cards printed "yet"—or they use old cards with parts crossed out. They say they're "exploring their options," or "taking some time off to think about things." Chances are they're standing with their shoulders drooped a little, and they'll answer your questions—especially business questions—with a stammer or a tentative response.

I don't mean to sound contemptuous of untrepreneurs—like I said, I was there myself not too long ago. But don't confuse your status if you're in the wrong category—your contacts and business prospects can spot the difference a mile away.

Rule Two: Be Prepared to Go Easy on Yourself. Sounds like the wrong advice, I know. Every *other* entrepreneurial book, magazine, course, and fortune-cookie sound bite o' wisdom tells you to prepare for hundred-hour workweeks, no sleep, and a social life best described as sluglike. And they're all correct: working for yourself means some major work, major stress, and major hours.

But at the same time, you can't expect yourself to work twenty-four hours a day, seven days a week, and still be standing at the end of the year. Evolution hardwired us with a range of physical and psychic needs, including food, sleep, socializing, and sex. You can't start a business and expect yourself to turn into the Terminator on Day One, or even day 1,001. Be sure to budget yourself a life in between your work. Otherwise, you'll be on the fast track to a serious burnout.

That having been said, you can't slack off either. Most folks get used to the imposed discipline of having to be in class at ten, or in the office at nine. When you're self-employed, you set your own start time, and if that happens to be at four in the afternoon after *Gilligan's Island,* you're toast. The snooze button is your mortal enemy. So is Joey Buchanan (or Commander Data). So is your best college buddy who wants you to join him in tequila shooters on a Tuesday night.

Entrepreneurship requires everything you've got, and sometimes a little more. You won't be living up to other people's expectations of you this time—it's up to you to decide just what one hundred percent effort is, and to live up to it. I'm personally convinced that most people know what their own energy levels are, and somewhere deep inside they know whether they're living up to their potential or falling short.

We'll talk more about the nuts and bolts of one hundred percent (and one hundred and ten percent) when we get to time management. But keep in mind that those are subjective terms: you choose what they mean, and then you determine from your successes and failures whether you're right. When you haven't seen your best friend in a month, you're pushing too hard. When you haven't made a dollar in a month, you're slacking off. I can recognize both because I've been both places—but if you know what to look for, you don't need to live through those pendulum swings to see where you're going.

I think most untrepreneurs are slackers, and most entrepreneurs are burnouts in training. If you're the latter, or trying to be, learn how to kick on your afterburners, and then learn how to shut them off.

Rule Three: The People Around You Are Only Human. One of the biggest pains in the ass to the new entrepreneur is that you're instantly surrounded by astonishingly successful self-made people. Just ask them, and they'll be sure to tell you how they always return phone calls within ten minutes of the message, how their in box is empty, how their filing system is perfect, and how they billed exactly 168 hours last week.

The zenith of this kind of thing is in Tony Robbins's book *Awaken the Giant Within*. He kicks off with a paragraph that says:

> I'll never forget the day it really hit me that I was truly living my dream. I was flying my jet helicopter from a business meeting in Los Angeles, traveling to Orange County on the way to one of my seminars. . . . I suddenly recognized a

A story was going around the Internet a while ago about some total schmuck in Arizona who had no idea what he was getting himself into. Apparently, this Einstein decided that he wanted to drive *really fast*. So he somehow laid his hands on a solid-fuel Jet-Assist Takeoff (JATO) booster rocket, which he then soldered onto the underside of his Chevy. Then he found himself a really long, straight road, and set the rocket off.

Now, this guy was smart enough to smuggle military hardware. He was smart enough to attach the rocket to his car so that it didn't blow apart the car when it went off. And he knew to do this out in Arizona, which is basically just long expanses of sand broken up by the occasional retirement community—the inhabitants of which must have been very amused to see a Chevy blow by at three hundred miles per hour.

This guy was clueless, however, on two key factors. One, the JATO rocket has no off switch. Two, Chevys aren't supposed to go much over sixty, and their brakes and steering wheels tend to fail at ICBM cruising velocities. Which is why the guy was scraped off the side of a small hill with a putty knife.

The moral of the story? Hell, it doesn't really need one. But if I had to say, it's a case of classic half-assed burnout.

large building, and I stopped the helicopter and hovered above it. As I looked down, I realized that this was the building I'd worked in as a janitor only twelve years ago!

Jet helicopter. Yeah, right. I'll be glad to lay it on the line for you: I don't own a jet helicopter. I doubt I could even afford to rent one.

What Robbins is trying to do, of course, is psych his readers into a self-confident frenzy. (And he's remarkably successful, which is why his book appears on my recommended list.) The problem is that this same sort of personality is frequently what you encounter in clients, prospects, and competitors. There's not much that's more disheartening than meeting one of these propeller-heads going after the same customers as you are, when your office is an old refrigerator box. You look at him and say, "He's got style, experience, and he never misses a beat. What the hell am I doing?"

Here's what you've got to remember: entrepreneurs, by definition, are consummate bullshit artists. They take their own thoughts, ideas, and concepts and turn them into reality, for which people then throw money at them. That takes equal parts substance and style. Coming up against it can be extremely intimidating for the newcomer—especially when your competition is thirty years older and has a decade more experience at being self-employed.

What this means for you is that you've got to have the substance, but you also have to pull off the style. It means deliberately getting in over your head once in a while, and knowing how to deal with it. But if you believe everything you hear from your competition, you'll feel like you're in over your head right from the start. Don't let that get to you.

I'm deliberately writing this book showing "warts and all." Every book I read when I was starting out held up the authors as paragons of business—and likewise made me feel a little less able to pull off a business myself. I'm not going to do that to you. I still make a lot of mistakes, and I don't live up to all of my ideals, but I do well enough to meet my own standards of success. Likewise for you, it's OK to make a few mistakes. Your competition is only human, as are you. Minimize your mistakes and learn from them, and you'll stand a hell of a better chance than if you expect too much or too little from yourself.

Rule Four: Hire Yourself. You've been trained for years to put your best foot forward during job interviews. You know that you get butterflies in your stomach on the first day of a job, and that you can channel that nervous energy into doing better work. Ever since your first day in an industrial age educational institution, they've been hammering all of these learned responses into you so that you salivate at the sound of a work gong.

So why ignore these traits? Exploit them. Put away the Corn Pops and burn the sweats. Hire yourself to be CEO of your own company. Use the Abyss-Hack-Success worksheet as your job interview. Write out your salary and benefits demands—they'll be good later as either a benchmark or a belly laugh. And show up for work on the day you choose as Day One, with the appropriate body parts shaven, in good business clothes, even if you're not meeting anyone more important than your goldfish.

Why do this? Because you have to learn how to build a mind-set. People who work for someone in an honest-to-goodness office environment have the benefit of living creatures to help them through the workday. Their office is their Skinner box, and over the course of the day, external stimuli—deadlines, lunch breaks, Dilbert cartoons, sexual harassment, what have you—get pumped in. This results in various proactive and reactive behaviors, which result in a paycheck and bennies, et cetera, et cetera.

Unfortunately, you don't start off with an environment. Or, at least, think scorched earth—you're out there all by your lonesome. Later, we'll figure out the details of partners, employees, consultants, and other ways to add more critters to your life, but keep in mind that if you're running your business, or even if you're just the co-boss, you have to take charge of many things on your own. The reactive Skinner box personality has got to go.

Fortunately, you're human, so you've been hard-wired with two innate responses that go off without the benefit of coworkers, and which you can use to bootstrap yourself into your own business. They're called free will and hunger. Use both of these the way Nature intended, and that's all you'll need.

That's what you need to bring to your first day on the job, along with nice clothes and a good behind-the-ears cleaning. Or whatever it takes to psych yourself up. The first day of a new job is supposed to be a big deal—don't blow this one.

As for what you should actually do on your first day, I recommend the next chapter, where we'll figure out exactly what your business is going to be and how you'll make a living. Perhaps today's a good day to be Day One. Or maybe you want to take some more time to let all of this percolate. What you're thinking of doing is a big step—try working on that life-plan worksheet I mentioned if you're still unsure about this.

I f you're *still* confused, skim the rest of this book to see what you're in for, then get your hands on a copy of Barbara Sher's *I Could Do Anything If I Only Knew What It Was.* It's the best book I've ever seen on figuring out what to do when you grow up.

CHAPTER 3

What to Do Before You Start

A few years ago, I was ensconced in my dorm room when there was a knock at my door. Since I lived in the crime-free environment of west Philadelphia (which is somewhat less dangerous than a World War I trench), I yelled to whoever it was to come right in, since the door was unlocked and I was too busy to be polite.

In walks Dirk, a Canadian friend of mine, who takes one look at me and my room and starts laughing his head off. I didn't quite realize what a tableau I presented until that particular moment.

On my couch, where I was lying, was a stack of "how-to-do-it" entrepreneurial books. To my right was my Power-Book, which at the moment was scanning through a few Internet discussion groups on running a business. On the floor was another Mac with my running set of notes and ideas. Next to the Mac were more books and back issues of

Inc., Entrepreneur, and *Success* magazines. Those were spread out next to my workbook from the Wharton Small Business Development Center (SBDC), my bulk pack of bound xeroxes from the "Business Basics" SBDC class, and a few other books I had checked out of the library. Off in a corner, collecting dust, was my classwork.

Hey, you've got to set your priorities straight.

I might have gone a bit overboard in my research, but I wanted to know everything there was to know about what I was getting myself into. Of course, it was all secondhand, and I knew there are some things you can't learn from books. But I figured the more I got into what I was doing, the more likely I was to be successful at it.

Later, Dirk told me that that was when he realized I was actually serious about this. And, in truth, the whole process had the effect of convincing *myself* that I was serious about it, which was far more important.

Now, the problem was that ninety percent of what I read was crap. The other ten percent repeated itself endlessly from book to book to bulk pack (but I'm thickheaded enough that maybe rereading it that much was a good idea). In any case, what I'm about to do is boil down about 30,000 pages of text, 8,000 e-mail messages, and three years of experience into one concentrated dose of helping you figure out what to do next.

> Sturgeon's Law: ninety percent of everything is crap. Corollary: There's no guarantee that the other ten percent isn't crap, either. Porten's Observation: With competition like this, there's always a market for quality.

Step One: Bliss Quest

Most people are surprisingly unaware of what truly makes them happy. They have vague notions that certain activities are more enjoyable than root canals and limb amputations, but if they had to pick out one thing that would give them great pleasure to pursue, they'd be stumped. It's even more flummoxing if you try to think of things you like to do that actually can make you some money.

So let's put the money part aside for a while. Take your favorite writing implement and some paper, and spend about five minutes brainstorming ideas—activities you enjoy, skills you have (business or personal), or even just ways you usually blow off your time.

If you've never tried to brainstorm before, here are the rules: you're not allowed to stop until the five minutes are up. You're not allowed to criticize anything you come up with—just write it down and go on to the next thing. Entries like "walking in the rain" and "gargling in public" are not to be skipped for being too silly. A brainstorm isn't a critique session, it's a creativity tool.

Here's what a typical brainstorm for this typical self-employed author might look like:

working with computers
drinking coffee
video games involving mindless carnage
socializing
comic books
spy fiction
history and American civilization
Internet

communications technologies
gadgets and gizmos
Democratic politics
liberal causes
get-out-the-vote campaigns
political campaigns
pinball
gambling
walks in the park
Star Trek
eating
newspapers
Web surfing
poker
card-playing
writing fiction
writing essays
academic research for short papers
occasional poetry
bad late-80s techno music
magazines and journals
Macintosh evangelism
travel
international conferences
scientific issues
ethics in science
global governance
United Nations support

OK, that's quite a mélange. Think of it as "life gumbo." Somewhere in there are the things that I made into my own business. Somewhere in your list are the things that you can make into yours.

Go back over your list, and this time put a star next to anything you're particularly good at. Remember, you're not yet thinking in terms of what can be useful for business—just in terms of what you can do well. In my case, I'm very good at remembering obscure technical details from *Star Trek* episodes, so that one gets a star. Likewise, my occasional poetry has been reviewed with glowing remarks by people I respect, so that one gets a star too. On the other hand, while I'm a supporter of the United Nations, I haven't done anything that I can think of that qualifies as "doing something well," so that gets skipped.

If you come up with new entries while you're thinking about your list, by all means toss them on the end. You're still at a point where all ideas are potentially good ones.

Now take a look at your list, especially the starred entries. Take out another sheet of paper, and write down a problem for each item. That is, write down something that gets in the way of your enjoyment of the activity, or some flaw in the products involved, or anything that keeps this particular part of your world from being totally perfect. You want to look at each item from all angles. Consider not only what is a problem for you, but what might be a problem for other people *and that you know how to solve.*

Step Two: Think Like a Mercenary Bastard

This is one of those potentially life-changing exercises. And, quite possibly, it could be a change for the worse. If you're the type who's in touch with the oneness of humankind, the beauty of nature, and the interconnectedness of all living things, then you're going to *hate* this.

What you have to do now is think money. Think business. Think commerce. Forget everything else for a moment or two. Close your eyes, count to three, and open your eyes. What do you see?

If you've successfully put aside your holistic thinking what you're looking at right now is a product. The book you're reading, the chair you're sitting on, the floor the chair is on, the paint on the walls, the building the walls are holding up—even the tree that's planted on the sidewalk. Everything around you essentially boils down to products. Air might be free here, but in Japan they sell it for 1,000 yen a bottle.

And if all of the physical *things* are products, then the activities of getting them to you are services. Someone shipped the beans from Guatemala for your latte, someone else picked them (probably for a few pennies an hour), and someone else roasted them, although the only person you'll see is the one who grinds them up and tosses them into the Krups. Somehow, out of the three dollars you'll fork over, all of those people along the way are making their living.

None of this is anything that you didn't know before, but it's a rare thing to contemplate it. Everything you own, everything you use, every place you go, and a great number of things you do all boil down to money changing hands. Ponder this long enough, and you'll start to miss the Communists—for most members of our generation, this is a pretty cold way to look at the world.

But from a business point of view, it's what you have to do—at least sometimes. Once you start to look around, and see just *how much* there is going on around you—the vast number of professions, jobs, and business opportunities that the economy creates—it's hard to believe that there isn't *something* out there for which you're perfectly suited.

As I've suggested, there are two basic methods for an entrepreneur to make money: products and services. The product business and the service business are two very different animals (although most entrepreneurs get involved in both eventually), so it's worth taking a look at the underlying principles of each one.

A product-based entrepreneur takes some sort of raw material and converts it into a finished product. That product might be in the ultimate final form that the consumer at the end of the line will buy, or it might be something that someone else will then convert into the final product. So if I invent a new children's clay using Vaseline, grape jelly, and my microwave, I can either go the whole route and package it in plastic eggs, then sell it at Kmarts around the country— or I can sell it in 1.6-cubic-foot batches to someone else, who will take it to the final market.

Usually, the amount of money a product-based entrepreneur makes is based on the amount of goods he sells, provided he's smart enough to charge a profit on what he sells. It's amazing how many people manage to miss this step— no joke.

A service-based entrepreneur, on the other hand, sells time rather than products. A service boils down to anything you can do, or that you can get someone else to do, that someone will pay you for. Naturally, not all services are legal, but we'll assume for the sake of argument that the ones you may be considering won't land you in jail.

The beauty of a service-based business, and the reason why so many people drift into those unmentioned illegal services, is that all you need is a client. With products, you have to start out with raw materials, end up with finished materi-

There's a classic Monty Python sketch where Eric Idle approaches John Cleese, marketing consultant. Idle tells Cleese that he's inherited a long piece of string—"a hundred thousand miles of it, in fact . . . all in three-inch lengths." Cleese goes on to improvise a series of uses—tying things to pigeons' legs, or wrapping very small parcels.

High comedy, I thought. Then I found out a friend of mine had a grandfather who did very well by his family when his string factory landed a contract to sell two-inch bits of string to a tea-bag manufacturer.

Totally ludicrous—and very lucrative.

als, have a place to store them, and be able to schlep them to where you make the sale. With services, it's more or less all in your head. It might take some refining to make your diamond-in-the-rough skills into a professional service, but once you do that, then *you're* the product. Service-based work requires almost no money to get started, and very little money to sustain the business during its early period when it probably won't bring in much revenue.

That's a major reason why I'm a consultant, living primarily off of services. But you shouldn't think in terms of products or services. What you're holding in your hands is a product, which is my venture into the other side of entrepreneurship. The publisher paid me first for the service of writing the book, but I also get a share of the sale of the product—this particular copy of the book—in its final form, even though someone else did all the work of getting it to you.

This is a pretty important part of being an entrepreneur— constantly watching for new opportunities or new products and services. What I'm doing in writing this book is totally different from what I do with my clients—but it all fits under the umbrella of entrepreneurship. And the idea came to me when I was in mercenary bastard mode and noticed that there was book that hadn't yet been written that I knew how to write.

Being a mercenary bastard gives you a new way of looking at commerce, and how you can snag your share of it. Sniff out the way money moves from one person to another, and watch for ways you can become a part of those transactions, either by providing the products that flow into the pipeline, or the service of moving products or information from one place to another. The more you watch how other people are making money, and the more you notice the number of ways this takes place, the quicker you'll find your own niche.

Step Three: Inventing the Job

Let's take a hypothetical example involving the worst possible activity, and try to turn it into a business. Our friend Joe

The problem with slipping into mercenary bastard mode is that some people get very comfortable there and decide to stay. I've met a fair number of people who see those around them as nothing more than conduits to moving money into their pockets. Some of them are financially successful, but I wouldn't want to have lunch with them, and I avoid doing business with them whenever possible.

Being in business means that sometimes you have to reduce things to monetary terms. Thinking about people and objects solely in terms of currency, however, leaves out of the equation most of what makes them worthwhile. Forget that, and entrepreneurship is going to suck you dry worse than any boss ever did.

has spent the last six months watching television. His apartment is unfurnished, with the exception of a twenty-seven-inch television set, a four-head VCR, and an eight-year-old futon that has seen better days. His job search went nowhere, partially because he spent too much time slacking off and partially because he didn't hear about anything good.

Joe is reading the newspaper one day and comes across a blurb in the Style section about people hating their VCRs. One person interviewed says, "I've never been able to figure the thing out. I have it turned around to face the wall so I don't have to stare at that blinking 12:00 all the time." Someone else mentioned, "I can tape shows until the cows come home, but I never have time to watch them anyway, so what's the point?" A third goes on, "Between cable and satellite and all of those high-tech features, I'm ready to just junk everything except my five-inch black-and-white set."

Joe's been thinking about trying to get some money to supplement the Kraft macaroni-and-cheese diet he's been on, and his wheels start turning. If Joe's not particularly bright, at this point he might think, "Hey, I can start a service where I set people's VCR clocks for them, so they don't flash 12:00!" Thanks to daylight saving time, Joe might get repeat business twice a year, but it's questionable whether people would be willing to pay for this.

If Joe is a little bit smarter, he might think, "I can tape shows for people who can't program their VCRs, so they don't worry about missing their shows. I can even chop out the commercials for them, so they don't have to fast-forward all the time." Now Joe may or may not be on to something— it depends on how many people would be interested in this kind of service.

But if Joe's neurons are really in a frenzy, he'd say, "I live in Washington, D.C. (or New York, or Los Angeles), where people are totally news-fixated. I can tape all of the news shows, prepare a list of what stories were aired, fax it to a list of clients, and give them tapes upon request of only what they want to see, saving them time and keeping them informed!"

Or he might take another tack and say, "I'll hire myself out to wealthy people who want to buy great home-entertainment systems but don't know what to get. I'll be the informed third party, more trusted than a salesman, who picks out the best package for the client and sets it all up for them."

Unfortunately, Joe's a typical untrepreneur, so he sits on his butt and eventually forgets about his ideas halfway through his third bag of microwave popcorn.

Are any of Joe's ideas good? There's no way of knowing—we're just in the idea-generation stage at this point. But Joe managed to come up with four different business ideas, starting with his TV and VCR.

If Joe's the type to read newspapers instead of watch TV, maybe he'd have thought of a daily news synopsis of six major newspapers. Or special gloves that won't get newspaper ink on your hands when you read. Or an easel that lets you read a full-sized paper while you use a knife and fork.

And if Joe's a sports fanatic, maybe he'd . . . well, hell, I don't know jack about sports. But you get the idea.

There's not much out there that can't inspire new products and services. It's just a matter of seeing something that other people overlook and acting on it. The mercenary bastard approach, in which you follow the money, will usually lead you to one set of destinations, while a more holistic view of the world may lead you to another.

Take some time to review your master list of skills and interests. If those don't lead you to any ideas, try thinking about the problem backwards. What are the obvious needs in your community? Is the grocery store ten miles from the retirement community whose residents can't drive? Does the video store deliver, or carry Jackie Chan martial arts flicks? Are there any products that you have to buy from catalogs because no one nearby sells them? Are the catalogs all made in small print? When you talk with people in your community, what do they usually complain about?

Make a list of these things, then see if any ring a bell with your skills and interests.

And if *that* doesn't work, put your list away for a week, sit down, and try again from scratch. Then compare both lists. See what new things you can come up with.

If brainstorming still leaves you dry, plagiarize. Spend time at malls, in business districts, reading the phone book and the ads in the newspapers. Figure out what other businesses are going on around you, and if there are any you can duplicate. Strict mimicry is a very dangerous game, since you'll be going up against businesses that are already established—but perhaps thinking about how you'd do *exactly* what someone else is doing might get you started on something more inventive.

Step Four: Fallbacks

OK, now after all that work, you've finally got your business idea. Your next step: start over.

At this point, it's impossible to know whether your idea is a good one. The more alternatives that come to mind, the better off you'll be in case your first one turns out to be less profitable than you had hoped.

What you're really looking for in the way of fallback ideas are businesses that you can switch to, if necessary, without significantly changing what you're doing or how you're doing it. You'll have already built up a set of skills and resources for the first business idea; now what other things can you do with those same abilities?

My first business idea was to be an all-around computer consultant. I scrapped that pretty early on in favor of being a consultant specifically for users of Macintosh computers. My fallback was as a secretarial rent-a-helper, since I already had the portable computer and an espresso-fortified typing speed. As it turned out, my consulting business took off well enough for me to dump the secretarial work as soon as I realized that any client who saw me as a secretary would pigeonhole me there for the rest of my life. But it put food in my belly for a crucial few months.

Fallbacks mean flexibility. Flexibility means food. Food is good. For a business start-up, that's a reasonable goal while you're learning what you're doing.

CHAPTER 4

Getting Down to Business

*W*hen you start a business, you have to hammer down a lot of details.

For instance, you'll have to follow guidelines, set by Uncle Sam, regarding how the business is organized, who is in charge, and who gets taxed. Also, for the sake of your own sanity, you'll also have to establish certain internal structures that will provide you with clear ideas as to who your supporters and helpmates are and where the business is heading.

There are two parts to developing your business structure. The first is to determine the form of your business—its legal identity—and whether it exists totally on its own or is dependent on a network of other businesses. The second is to draw up a business plan, which we'll tackle in chapter 6.

The good news is if you've been worried about doing everything on your own, there are ways to affiliate yourself with a larger group of other businesses, all of which will have

Internet

Why You Need to Be on the Internet

There's another world out there. It goes by a variety of confusing names: the Internet, cyberspace, America Online, CompuServe, the World Wide Web, and others.

Most people of our generation usually fall into two groups: the ones who have been online and can't get enough of it, and the ones who touch computers only when they have to and can't see the point of being involved with something as sterile as an electronic mail message.

This interlude is for the people in the latter category. The Internet has been called the wave of the future by media hacks who don't know any better. It's more than that—it's the most powerful tool on the planet for anyone who wants information about any topic, who wants an impartial sounding board, or who wants to tap into a pool of experts with more experience and, frequently, more wisdom and years under their belts.

I'll admit it right off—I'm a computer fanatic. I've been using computers since I was five, and the first model I ever used is now on display at the Smithsonian. When I was in college, they were a serious hobby; now they're my business and my livelihood. When the Internet took the world by storm, I needed no convincing to go exploring.

You've heard about the Internet. You've probably been confused by terms like the World Wide Web, or USENET, or 28,800-baud MNP5 send-receive fax modems. Or perhaps you've been dazzled by hype and glamour about the Information Superhighway.

Put all that aside. There is one reason and one reason alone why you need to be online. Thirty million people are already there. That's all there is to it.

continued

Among those thirty million people are thousands who have started their own businesses, or who have thought about it. There are thousands of experts with information you need, whether you know it yet or not. There are libraries with millions of pages of information that you can find with a little legwork or with the help of someone else who has been there before you. There are computer programs that you can grab for free and then use to help you with your business. There are friends and business contacts whom you can reach by electronic mail instead of running up your phone bills. And, lastly, there are potential clients and customers whom you'll never find any other way.

The Internet is the world's largest information resource, and the grandest human community in our collective history. You are foolishly handicapping yourself if you don't tap into it.

I'll be listing noteworthy online resources throughout the following pages. Each resource will be short, sweet, and utterly confusing if you're not familiar with the online world. Don't panic. You'll find more information about what it all means when we hit the technical information in chapter 7. If you don't understand it now, just ignore the online stuff until you're up to speed; all of the resources I list are collected in appendix A. If you're already wired, feel free to start digging into these resources as soon as I mention them—you'll find a lot of information that I can't include here, and maybe even a few people who disagree with me.

And if you just can't get enough of me, or you want to get more straight information after the book is published, drop me a line at creative@getnet.com. I'll send you periodic updates and useful information, zapped straight to you by electronic mail. I'll also have a lot of useful information at the Web site for this book at http://getnet. com/~ creative.

a vested interest in helping you succeed. The price is money and some of your freedom, but it might be worth it in return for some guidance.

We have three big picture questions before us in this chapter: 1) Should you quit your current job to leap into this headfirst? 2) Should you be completely independent, or join a network of businesses, or start a franchised business? 3) How should you define your business in the eyes of the government for tax and legal matters?

Selling Your Soul for a Little Longer

It's a given at this point that you're not satisfied with your present job. But it might just be the best place for you to be for a little while. There's a lot to be said for money in the bank.

There's an inevitable groundwork-laying period when you start a business. The standard rule of thumb is that it takes a business three years to start making a profit. That doesn't mean that you personally won't make any money for three years—business profit is counted only *after* the principal (that is, you) gets his or her salary paid from the entrepreneurial venture. But it's worth noting that, given a usual business growth curve, you won't see serious bucks for a few years— even if there's no difference between your "salary" and the business profits.

For you, the entrepreneur, there's another basic rule for how much you'll make if you start a business. This coming year, you'll make a lot less than you made working for someone else. The second year, you'll make about the same amount of money. The year after, you'll start making more—maybe substantially more.

Unfortunately, the promise of money in three or four years isn't worth a Big Mac right now. And without money, you might very well be reduced to begging for Big Macs. Money is the only reward for a lot of bad jobs, and it's not enough—but it becomes a lot more important when you don't have any.

On the other hand, it's substantially more difficult to start a business when you're giving a large chunk of your waking hours to an employer. Working for someone else, there will always be more reasons coming up to stay at work for just one more month, making it that much harder to finally leave.

So, what's the best option? The answer depends on the following questions:

> *Are Your Basics Covered?* If you run out of money, will you continue to have a place to live and food to eat? Or are you risking homelessness and hunger if you don't have any cash?

> *Do You Have Any Savings?* Without income, will your debts get paid off—if not on time, then at least frequently enough to prevent collection agencies from repossessing your life?

> *Are Your "Essential Luxuries" Paid For?* Earlier, you listed the things in your life that you weren't willing to live without—the "man does not live by bread alone" luxuries that have become necessities for you. Are these fully paid up, or are some of them dependent on your next paycheck?

It would not be at all out of the ordinary for your business not to produce a dime for you for three months—and even longer if you have to invest much money to get started in the first place. If you have enough squirreled away to make a go of it with no additional income for as long as it might take, or if there's someone willing to take on your expenses for a few months, then you might not need to report to work again.

When I started my business, I had not a dime to my name. But my parents had fully stocked my fridge, and they had agreed that I could call them when a major bill came due that I couldn't cover. They covered my rent for a good five months right off the bat, and occasionally thereafter. Without that sort of support, it would have been foolish for me to start when I did. I would have had to take a job for a year and put away the money I needed to do what I really wanted to do.

In chapter 8 we'll go over some ways of supplementing your income through part-time jobs and other more creative methods, so that it won't be one hundred percent necessary to have a nest egg large enough to eat omelets forever. But if you have full-time income coming in right now, consider whether it wouldn't be smarter to stick it out a little while longer, with the express intent to save as much dough as you can.

There are two apparent reasons to bail on your job even if it leaves you in a tricky financial situation. First, if your business idea is extremely time-sensitive, meaning that if you don't jump on it immediately, it's going to either disappear or someone else is going to do it. Second, if you suspect that staying in your current job "to make money for later" is really just an excuse to stay where it's safe and not risk the entrepreneurial plunge.

Both of these are sound reasons to leave a job, but they also show serious weaknesses in your business idea. If the business is so precarious that it might be financially unsound in three months, then is it really worth risking a longer-term investment of your life in it? And if you suspect that you're staying in your job because you're afraid to strike out on your own, then that's exactly where you should be until you know for certain whether you have the fire in the belly to take on this kind of risk.

Working a full-time job until you've gotten yourself together is, without a doubt, the prudent, responsible thing to do. But it's not what I did—and although I paid for it later in stress (and my parents paid for it in money), I'm happy that I took the plunge. A full-time job and salary looked pretty good during the bad times of my first year; if I had gotten used to that kind of security once, I might have gone back to it like an unrecovered, thrice-quit cigarette addict.

How to Be on Your Own Without Going Alone

If you're sold on being your own boss, but less clear on how exactly you can pull it off or whether you've got the skills to make it up from scratch, you might want to consider starting a business that's actually part of a bigger business. The two most common ways of doing this are through business franchises (such as Domino's Pizza) and multilevel marketing companies (of which Amway and Mary Kay are the best known).

Getting a Piece of the (Pizza) Pie

The basic idea behind a franchise operation is that you buy from a central company the right to use their logos, products, and marketing; in return you get the right to run a store with their name, which you have more or less complete control over within the guidelines of the company.

Let's take McDonald's as a hypothetical example. Why hypothetical? Because starting a new Mickey D's can run you a cool quarter million dollars. That's what you need to shell out to buy the franchise rights to the name, and build a store to their specifications with their fixtures and kitchen equipment. What you get out of it is ownership of a burger joint, a stack of training manuals and information about making a McDonald's successful, and a month's training at (no joke) Hamburger U.

Now all you have to do is run your store. But make sure you don't break any McRules, which can be substantial. McDonald's keeps close tabs on its franchisers to make sure that every McDonald's from Minneapolis to Minsk looks and tastes more or less identical. If you're dreaming of selling McSteaks or adding a black-tie dress code, McDonald's can come in and take back all of their spatulas.

But if you're willing to toe the line, you do get to run your own business. A percentage of your proceeds will get kicked back to the company as per your contract, so you don't keep all the loot, but then again you get to have your business advertised by Michael Jordan and Bugs Bunny.

Franchising is a great way to start a business because a lot of the work has already been done for you. Most of the big names go for the big bucks, but you can pick up dozens of businesses for less than $1,000. Of course, in many cases you'll get what you pay for: a low-cost franchise might come with a mere hundred-page manual, if that, and little support down the line.

If you want to explore this further, the best place to start is *Entrepreneur* magazine's annual "best franchises" issue. They rank thousands of franchises based on costs, kickback requirements, and managerial support, and let you know what to expect when you get started. The 1996 issue was published in January; check a local library or call *Entrepreneur* at (714) 261-2325.

Multilevels: The '90s Version of Pyramid Power

The other way to go into this with tons of support is to get involved in a multilevel marketing company. Multilevel marketing (frequently called MLM) lets you make money not only from the products you sell, but also from the products *other* people are selling.

Here's how it works: once you've been recruited into an MLM, you have two jobs. First, sell the product. Second, recruit *other* people to sell the product. These people nominally work for you, but are also considered to be entrepreneurial distributors and are as self-employed as you are. You're supposed to show them the ropes and help them get started; in return, the company keeps track of everyone you've recruited and gives you a share of the profits from their sales.

What makes this even better is that you also get a share of the profits from the sales of your recruits' recruits, and so on and so on. This is referred to as your "downline," which is basically your company family tree. You and your downline are part of someone else's downline, as well; travel far enough up your upline in an established MLM, and you'll find stacks of multimillionaires who have been raking in the bucks from their steadily growing downlines for decades.

There are MLMs for just about every product under the sun. The granddaddy of them all is Amway, which has been around since the 1950s and has sales reps scattered all over the globe. Amway's product listings encompass six catalogs and range from food to office supplies to new cars. If your taste is more feminine, check out Mary Kay Cosmetics, which made a name for itself by giving away pink Cadillacs to its top sellers. For the New Agers among you, Nikken sells a variety of magnetic mattresses, pillows, and chairs that supposedly get your blood in alignment, or something like that. And on and on.

So what's the catch? Most MLMs require new sales reps to purchase a start-up kit, which is typically a set of manuals and some sample products. Of course, you're supposed to turn around and sell those products and recoup your costs—but there's still going to be some money required to jump in. Some MLMs are better about this than others: Amway's starter kits come with enough product to turn a profit when you sell it all, but others can leave you in the hole for hundreds of dollars.

The odd part about MLMs is that the real money isn't in selling the products, it's in recruiting other people to sell in your downline. If you sell a lot of products, you'll do all right. But if you sell only a few products and recruit a lot of people who move warehouse loads, then you'll be sitting on top of a pile of money.

Here's what one sales rep, who's involved with a major MLM, told me was his company's path to riches. First, meet fifteen to twenty new people a week and invite them to a presentation about the company. Actually make this presentation to about five people a week. Do this for the next two to five years. At the end of that time, given normal attrition in your downline, you should be making a six-figure salary from downline sales.

Sounds great, and pretty quick. But check out that hidden catch: meeting twenty people every week and constantly asking everyone you know to come to a presentation. This requires the relentlessness of the Terminator to pull off. But people have done it, and maybe you already know a lot of people to start pumping into your downline.

You probably see ads for MLMs daily: those classified ads and flyers that say, "Make $500–$2,000 a week from your home," without giving any indication of *what* you'll be doing, are probably MLMs. You can also find many advertised, again, in *Entrepreneur* magazine.

If you think this is your cup of java, here's what to look for, and look out for, in MLM companies:

Reliability and Duration. You want your company to be around a few years from now; there's no value in a down-line when the company goes bust. Amway is probably the odds-on favorite to outlast our grandchildren, but be careful—the older the company, the more likely they've already saturated your area with sales reps.

Low-Cost Entry Fees. Every company is going to charge you *something,* since the great majority of their reps sign up and never buy anything but the starter kit. They need to make enough profit off you right off the bat to make you worth their time. But if the charges are too high, that's an indication that the company is making its money by soaking their sales reps, not by legitimate business practices.

Training and Support. There's no point in getting on board with an MLM if they're not going to teach you something about how to recruit and move the product. You want to make sure there's an adequate support system behind you. But also beware of getting sucked in. Some MLMs run frequent seminars at $400 a pop or better. At those rates, it's possible to toss every dime you make right back into the corporate coffers. Make sure that seminars aren't *required* for participation.

Product Value. Don't hop on board until you've actually seen what you'll be selling, or at least heard from a reliable source that the products are worthwhile. (A reliable source is a user of the product who is not also *selling* the product!) Again, Amway and Mary Kay have proven track records here, but don't buy the hype of a company you aren't already familiar with.

Legal Business Practices. MLMs frequently get a bad rap, and sometimes deservedly so, since their sales reps are so driven to proselytize the product and recruit new members. It's a bizarre cross between entrepreneurship and the Moonies. I've been to MLM support meetings that felt like Hitler youth groups with shampoo instead of swastikas.

One area in which they've gotten a great deal of scrutiny is their methods of profiting. The federal government has taken great pains to make sure that MLM operators don't run Ponzi, or pyramid, schemes. The Ponzi scheme dates back to an inventive crook in the 1920s who offered his clients ludicrously high returns on their investments with him, something like twenty percent a month. Early investors got exactly the return they were promised, because Ponzi took the money from the second dozen investors and used it to pay off the first dozen. The third dozen went back to the second, and so on. So long as he got new investors, everything was fine. But the plan is doomed to failure—at some point you simply run out of new people, at which point a lot of people go bankrupt if they've put all their money into this "investment."

The U.S. government was concerned enough about the possibility of that happening that they ruled Ponzi schemes absolutely, totally, one hundred percent illegal, with the sole exception of the mandatory Social Security system, which is based upon exactly the same principle. Early MLMs didn't have the benefit of government sanction, however, so the Securities and Exchange Commission got involved with their dealings. The result: a few were shut down because essentially the only thing they were selling was memberships, in elaborate extensions of the Ponzi system.

To be a legit MLM, all moneys that are paid have to eventually be traceable to the sale of some product. If the money can't be tracked down in that fashion, the whole thing could very well be illegal and shut down, leaving you once again with a zilched-out downline. If you have any questions about the legality of an MLM, contact the SEC at (202) 942-8088. For more information about a particular MLM's business practices, longevity, or reliability, ask a librarian at a public or college library to do a search for legal proceedings against the company, and look up newspaper and magazine articles that review their business. If an MLM has never appeared in reputable print, that's a danger sign right there. You can also look into whether the business has ever gotten negative reviews at your local Better Business Bureau or Chamber of Commerce, but since many of those are run by businesspeople themselves,

Internet

A great place to find out more about MLMs in general or one in particular is the USENET group misc.business.multilevel. More information can also be found in misc.entrepreneurs.moderated. The misc.entrepreneurs group is usually flooded with MLM pitches, which makes it worthless for discussion but a useful place to go trolling for business offers. If you can't find a rep in your area for a particular MLM, drop me a line at creative@getnet.com.

it's sometimes questionable whether your results will tell you anything useful.

The Form of Your Business

There are millions of businesses in this country, but all of them fall into one of three categories: sole proprietorships, partnerships, and corporations. For most purposes, these distinctions will have little impact on how your customers interact with your company. But your choice will have a major impact on the complexity and costs of running your business.

Sole Proprietors: The Kid at the Lemonade Stand

The simplest form of business is a sole proprietorship. It's a long way of saying that one person is running his own business.

Legally, a business organized as a sole proprietorship is indistinguishable from the person who runs it. The business is a legal extension of yourself and has no separate existence. So if the business loses money, or gets sued, or runs into legal trouble, total responsibility falls in your lap.

As you might expect, the proprietor has total control over the sole proprietorship—the business is you, so you don't have to answer to anybody. You keep every dime that comes in, and you pay every penny that goes out.

Many small businesses start out this way, and it will be the most immediately attractive option for the majority who read this book. Sole proprietorships cost nothing to start, aside from the basic costs of starting the business—no legal fees, no accountant fees, and usually just a nominal licensing fee from

the local government. You can use your existing bank accounts and financial records, but you'll have to keep your
business expenses listed separately from your personal finances. Your business profits go onto your personal income
tax form; you might have to file different forms than you did
before, but they are still the same taxes that you've been
forced to get used to over the years.

Sole proprietorships aren't immune from other factors
that can complicate the life of a business owner, including hiring laws and insurance issues. It's the easiest way to start and
run a business, but that doesn't mean it's easy.

Partnerships—The Kid Joins His Sister and Takes Over the Block

If you're planning on going into business with someone else,
you'll probably be eyeing the partnership. Partnerships create
business entities that are then owned by all of the partners. In
the eyes of the law, they're treated as sole proprietorships that
are divided among several people. All profits, all debts, and all
responsibilities are shared by the partners according to the
terms of their agreements.

Partners in a business are bound by a set of agreements
that they draw up when the business is formed. The division
of ownership is usually based on the amount of money that
each ponies up, but frequently a number of percentage points
will be shifted based on "sweat equity"—the partner who does
more work gets more say.

When it comes time to render unto Caesar, the partnership itself pays no taxes, but it must file forms with the feds to
let them know how much the partnership paid each partner.

Partnerships have a unique set of strengths and weaknesses
that don't affect the sole proprietor. Since the business starts

off with the skills and experience of two or more people, it's got more going for it and more hands to do the work. There's also a shared sense of responsibility, which can be a great impetus to live up to your plans and expectations. A good partnership balances the partners' strengths and weaknesses.

The downside is the sharing of control of the business. The worst thing you can do is divide control equally among an even number of partners and just assume that you'll have consensus all along the line. Money matters and business fractures have broken up many friendships, relationships, and marriages over the years, and there's great harm in believing that you and your partners will be magically immune from serious disagreement.

Partnerships require much more rigorous examination and planning concerning business issues. Everyone involved has to have a shared understanding of where the business is going, how it's going to get there, who's going to drive, and who's going to pay for the gas. Brainstorm every possible reason for dispute and conflict among the partners, even a few that seem ludicrous now, so you don't get caught flat-footed when a disagreement comes down the pike later. If you can't reach consensus before the business is created, it's a fair bet that you're not suited to be business partners.

Partnerships require legal and accounting assistance in their formation and their annual tax filings. It's not a major task, but the hourly rates are high, so expect to sink a few hundred into professional fees.

Limited Partnerships— Mom Buys a Lemon Grove

A variation of the partnership is the limited partnership. A limited partner usually contributes only money to the partnership.

Limited partners may contribute expertise and, in rare cases, day-to-day operational help on a short-term basis, but final authority and all decisions are left up to the full partners.

A limited partner gets a piece of the action, but only a small amount of liability for business failures. While general partners have the same obligations to the business as sole proprietors, a limited partner loses only his investment money if the business goes belly-up.

Limited partnerships are a common method of financing businesses that require some start-up cash but that probably wouldn't qualify for bank loans. The partners flesh out the details of the business, approach their Uncle Joe (or some other family member or friend who might be a little more willing to listen than First National Bank), and he tosses in $1,000 or $100,000 in return for a share of the business and limited liability.

Limited partnerships, being a little more tricky, require a little more work from lawyers and accountants.

Corporations—The Kid Branches Out

Thanks to the wonders of modern legal technology, there are two ways to make a person in twentieth-century America. The old-fashioned way is to get (or get someone) pregnant. The new way is to form a corporation.

A corporation is legally a "fictitious person." It can own property, make money, pay taxes, get sued, and participate in most of the financial and legal proceedings that breathing human beings get subjected to. It can't vote, of course, but a few have been known to buy elections.

If you incorporate your business, you basically become your own employee. You own the company, which lists you as an employee. If you start the business with a few friends, they become employees, as well—working for the business, not directly for you.

The question of who owns and runs the business is determined by the incorporation charter. Typically, a corporation issues shares of private stock, which are traded internally rather than on a public stock exchange. Control of the company is shared by all stockholders, who vote on company issues in proportion to the amount of stock they hold. Day-to-day events are run by the company president or chief executive officer, while long-term strategies are set by the board of directors (of which the CEO may be the ranking member).

Creating a person is much easier the old-fashioned way than the new way. You don't need lawyers the old way. Forming a corporation, however, requires a stack of paperwork and forms that have to be pored over by an attorney and then filed with the appropriate local, state, and federal government agencies. This can run you some serious bucks. There are many lawyers who advertise that they'll set up a corporation for a flat fee of a few hundred dollars, but that only buys you a corporation with an internal structure based on boilerplate documents. If you want to customize the structure to suit your own needs, you'll be put on the clock. And the only way to know if you want to customize is to ask your lawyer and be put on the clock in the first place. According to my informal survey of prices that people on the Internet said they paid, the usual range is from $1,000 to $2,000 once everything is said and done.

The primary advantage of a corporation is its ability to legally separate the doings of the business from your own personal life. If the business goes bankrupt after it's paid you a few million in salaries and bonuses, you get to keep the thirty-foot sailboat so long as it's yours, not a business asset. When a sole proprietorship or a partnership goes bankrupt, it'll take the owners along with it.

And while it's not much of a concern for our age group, corporations outlast the life spans of their owners. If a sole proprietor or member of a partnership dies, agreements and contracts made by the company can go into limbo until the continuation of the company is determined. A corporation, being a separate entity, survives its owner and allows the transfer of ownership and shares to proceed in a less tumultuous fashion. This might not be the most important problem on your mind right now, but statistically speaking it's important to prepare for the chance of a bungee cord breaking.

Since corporations can have their own incomes, they also pay their own taxes. These are over and above what you'll pay on your personal income taxes for the salary or salaries you receive from the company. This tax structure effectively sets an income threshold—below it, you pay less tax as a sole proprietor; above it, you pay less tax as a corporation. This threshold has been estimated at around $70,000, but that will fluctuate widely depending on revisions to the tax code and the state in which you live.

Corporations, once formed, have to follow strict government guidelines for annual document preparation and form filing. Corporations are as hard to dismantle as they are to assemble, so there's no easy way of turning back. But as complex as incorporating may be—and as much as you're likely to spend on legal and professional fees—you'll also be well-protected from various business disasters.

It's worth noting that owning a corporation doesn't give you free rein to do as you please without regard for personal consequences. As the head of a corporation, you will be responsible to all of the shareholders, even if you own a majority of the stock. And nothing will protect you from civil and criminal proceedings for negligent or unlawful actions; you've got the responsibility to keep your nose as clean as a sole proprietor or partner.

Corporations come in two varieties, the standard C corporation and the S corporation. The S corporation is a hybrid of the C corporation and the sole proprietorship or partnership, merging the tax schedules of the latter with the limited liability of the former. Ask your attorney which one is appropriate for your business; numerous authors and Internet denizens have noted that the wrong choice can be very costly.

So, Which Way to Go, George?

Most of my clients and colleagues are sole proprietors. So am I. We all started out this way because it's the most obvious option for start-ups. I think most of us would have formed partnerships if we had had the right people.

I t's worth noting that incorporating can also be a key indicator of half-assed entrepreneurship. I was at a business luncheon a few years back where we all got thirty seconds to announce to the crowd the work that we did. One guy announced that he was about to become an "Inc.," and then squandered his time explaining the lame joke after he failed to get a laugh. I have no idea what his business was.

Some people incorporate because they think they won't be taken seriously otherwise, or because they want it as a dubious badge of honor. Your customers don't care—incorporate for internal reasons only.

The main reason to incorporate is to limit your liability. A notable exception among my colleagues is a friend who incorporated when he started a local newsletter. Publishing is the sort of business where you might get sued no matter what you say, and it was prudent of him to anticipate the possibility.

Arnold Goldstein makes the strongest argument I've seen for incorporation in his book _Starting on a Shoestring_. The following passage is an excerpt from the text:

> No chapter on risk-reducing strategies would be complete without mentioning that greatest of risk-reducers—the corporation. Many personal bankruptcies were needlessly caused by the failure of the business person to incorporate. From my viewpoint it's no contest. The limited liability benefits of the corporation overshadow other considerations. Any attorney who disagrees is an attorney without broad experience in handling business failures.

OK, so we know what Arnold thinks. There's no doubt he's right about the risk issue—incorporating is the responsible thing to do.

But again we come back to the issue of responsibility and the cost of reducing risk. Incorporation can add to a list of headaches and costs just when you need them least. And the question in your mind should be, just what is it you are protecting?

One of the major advantages of starting out young is that we've got little to lose. I'll assume that you are where I was when I started—fresh out of college, with a negative net worth thanks to credit card and student loan debts, no assets to speak of, and no dependents or family members to support. If I get sued for everything I have and have to declare bankruptcy, I'll lose a pile of gadgets and a really nice apartment.

It's not a pleasant prospect to consider, but it's a lot more survivable than losing a house when your kids are playing in the family room.

If you've got any financial assets that you can't afford to lose, then incorporation is probably the way to go. Without it, you're literally risking everything on the gamble that no customer will ever call a lawyer about you. But if you're coming into this with a fresh face and an empty bank account, sole proprietorship will tide you over until you have assets to protect. You can always incorporate later; it's much harder to dismantle a corporation and go back to just being yourself.

CHAPTER 5

The Basics of Raking in Cash

Setting a price for most entrepreneurs is a stab in the dark. If you're selling your brainpower, how much is an hour of your time worth? Look around and you'll see some consultants selling themselves for $15 an hour—$20 for a night in some parts of town. Other folks pull down $10,000 for a half-hour speech at a luncheon, and get free food to boot.

Pricing products is just as tough. Is your widget worth a little bit more than what it cost you in materials? How about $100 to a specialty widget collector? Or $2.95 as an impulse purchase at the supermarket checkout register?

The success of your business hinges on getting the right amount of money for your services. Ask for too little, and you can swim in business and still go broke. Ask for too much, and you'll have a hard time finding customers to buy from you.

The worst thing about setting a price is an underlying truism: your product or service has no inherent value or price. Take diamonds, which will set most of us back in the four figures over the course of our lifetimes. Why are they so valuable? It's not because they're pretty—you'll need an education and a magnifying glass to tell them apart from the cubic zirconia you can buy on television. It's not because they're the hardest substance on Earth, unless you plan on using your diamonds as a working tool in your new career as a cat burglar.

And—the kicker—it's not because they're rare. Diamonds are the result of millions of years of constant pressure on ordinary coal, as anyone knows who can remember seeing Superman make a diamond with his heat vision. There is a *lot* of coal lying around, and plenty of diamonds.

So, is the price high because all diamonds are still underground? Nope—the DeBeers diamond syndicate, the Russian government, and others have warehouses full of the things. Heavily guarded warehouses, of course.

So . . . what makes them worth money? Carefully controlled artificial scarcity. The world's diamond merchants agree on how many diamonds they're going to release to the world's markets from year to year. If any one of them flooded the market with everything in their inventories, the "natural" price of diamonds would fall to the point where you could buy a diamond-studded digital watch at a 7-Eleven for $8.95.

If the price of a valuable commodity like diamonds can fluctuate that much—enough so that an international diamond cartel has to carefully control its markets—then so can the markets in which your products and services are competing. Don't try to find the inherent price in your products. Instead, look for the best price that will make you the most money.

Bargain Basement Pricing— A Bad Idea

A fair number of entrepreneurs go into the market expecting that they have to beat their competition on price, and try to generate sales by undercutting the market rates.

This makes a lot of sense at first. Your competition has customer loyalty and a history of making sales. When you burst forth with your own product, what seems like the easiest way of convincing a customer to come to you instead? Just wave your product in the air and say that she'll save fifty cents, or five hundred dollars, by coming to your store instead of theirs. After all, why do the big stores spend thousands of dollars advertising sales?

The problem with that logic is that you're competing with the big stores. J.C. Penney doesn't care if its profits are off on item X if its advertising for item X increases foot traffic throughout the store, which in turn increases profits on everything else it sells. But when you set all of your prices to be lower than the next guy's, you're cutting your profits on all items indefinitely. Trimming your profits at the crucial starting stage can be the difference between survival and failure.

Would You Buy Caviar at Kmart?

Low prices equals low quality in most people's minds. You don't buy a Honda Civic for its engine power. Likewise, if you saw a new Porsche 911 on sale at the same price as a

Volkswagen, your first thought would be, "What the hell is wrong with that Porsche?"

Your products and services need to have a high value in the minds of your potential customers. In a perfect world, customers would blithely accept a high-quality service at a low price and not think that inexpensive means cheap. Unfortunately, all of us have gotten jaded from constant exposure to capitalism; not only are we sure there's no free lunch, but we also expect to be charged extra for ketchup.

For these reasons, a small business aimed at providing high quality at low prices is doomed to failure. That strategy can work in the multibillion-dollar megastores, where a low profit margin on individual products is ameliorated by moving mountains of goods. But the same strategy will rapidly turn a small business into no business.

So your other two options are low quality at a low price, and high quality at a high price. Which do you think is the more effective plan? If you're going to work at building a business, the least you can do is do it right—and then get paid for what you're worth.

Thoughts on Quality

Perhaps you've noticed that I've skipped the idea of low quality at a high price. That's because it's impossible—no one has ever made a dime with this strategy.

Yeah, right, you think, remembering those $200 acid-washed jeans you passed over that came pre-torn, pre-shrunk, pre-battered, and required a drawstring to keep from falling to your knees. Those jeans were the worst piece of clothing you'd ever seen—how can those be quality?

The key here is the definition of quality. By any normal human standards, jeans like that are worthless—better to buy a pair for a buck at Salvation Army. But to the customer who buys those jeans, they're not seeing rips and tears as defects. They're seeing product features in the name on the label and the statement the jeans make.

No one buys low quality. Shoddy goods at a low price are high quality for some customers. Your job as an entrepreneur is to determine what your customers define as quality, and meet those standards.

The Goalposts on the Price Playing Field

There are three numbers that you can use to come up with your prices and fees. Taken together, they'll provide a low, middle, and high figure to use as a range when pegging your prices.

What Will All This Run You? Your low number is the cost of your materials and the overhead costs of running the business. These divide into two categories: fixed costs and direct costs. A fixed cost is an expense that doesn't change no matter how much business you do—rent, for example. Direct costs are tied to the number of products you make, or the number of people you prospect. The greater the number of clients and products, the greater the direct costs. Direct costs affect the product-based entrepreneur more than those in services. We'll discuss this in more detail when we talk about pricing products.

A very important fixed cost that most entrepreneurs forget is their own salary. Unless you plan to work for free, decide what you want your time to be worth and factor it into your costs. A weekly salary should be divided by the number of products you expect to move in a week in a product-based business, or by the number of hours you expect to work in a services business.

What Does the Other Guy Charge? The second number to keep in mind when setting your prices is what your competitors are charging for similar services. In most situations, you'll discover that there is a range in prices depending on your competitors' clientele. In computer consulting, I know some guys who charge $15 an hour—their clients are mostly parents with small children. Others charge $150 an hour or better for corporate clients in New York.

Your competitive range may give you more guidance than mine did. Your price will probably land somewhere in the middle, unless you have compelling reasons to do otherwise.

Maxing Out. The top of your spread should be determined by the maximum the market will bear. Every product and service has a top price, beyond which you will make no sales. The top price almost certainly will not be the most profitable—you're better off with a dozen clients who pay $60 an hour than a single client paying $250. There's no simple way to determine the top value of your products, since most people have no clear idea at what cost they would stop buying something. But you can guess and re-fine this number over time, as you get more information from your prospects, customers, and competitors.

Getting Your Money's Worth in Services

As a service-oriented entrepreneur, you have only one thing to sell: your time and that of your staff. Time is an incredibly precious resource. For you, it's your sole means of making an income; for your clients, it's probably what they are ultimately trying to conserve by hiring you.

More so than in a product-based business, in services you'll squander your business if you squander your time. And, unfortunately, it's possible to do just that even if you're working extremely long, hard hours.

The Magic and Misery of Billable Time

When I started my business, I billed myself out at $25 an hour. I would mention this to friends still in college, and even a few graduated friends, and their eyes would widen: "Twenty-five an hour? Wow, I'm only making five and a quarter!" I'll admit, the first time someone gave me a check for $50 after two hours, I was pretty psyched.

Now, the problem is that you can't bill all your time. In fact, you'll be lucky if you bill half your time. Billing $25 an hour does not equate to $1,000 a week after a forty-hour workweek. Frequently it can mean $100 a week after a sixty-hour workweek.

Time that you don't spend on contract is time that you don't get paid. Every consultant and services entrepreneur puts in a fair amount of unpaid time.

So, how do you set an hourly rate? First you have to determine what you want to make over a long period of time, and determine how many hours you'll have to bill at a particular rate to make that much.

Let's set your salary at $26,000 a year. We can also say that a year is equal to 2,000 hours: 50 weeks times 40 hours a week. If you could bill out every hour of every working day, $13 an hour would be just fine.

But you can't. For the beginning entrepreneur, it's virtually impossible to land the kind of clients who'll keep you that busy. So let's estimate that of the 2,000 hours in a year, half of them will be spent as billable time. Then you need to charge $26,000 divided by 1,000 hours, which comes out to $26 an hour.

However, that doesn't include your expenses, or your taxes, or anything else that will take bites out of your income. Once you start working that into your take-home, you have to think about rates approaching $30 or $35 an hour.

And that's based on what is, frankly, a very generous estimate of billable time. How long it will take you to bill more than half your time will depend on the kind of work your clients ask you to do. In my case, I spent a long time concentrating on training services, for which most clients want you for only two or three hours. Add in travel time, and it becomes difficult to see more than two clients in one day. Even three years later, it's very rare for me to break 50 percent billable time based upon this kind of consulting work.

If you think $25 an hour sounds like a lot of money, check out the tax returns from my first year in business. Including the money I made as a temp during my half-assed stage, I cleared less than $10,000 that year—low enough to qualify for a tax credit on my return. Officially impoverished.

I f you're wondering what eats up all those hours that you won't be billing, it's all the things you have to do to land clients: phone calls, networking meetings, small projects that you're doing for free in expectation of more paying work later, planning, returning messages and e-mails, and reading and researching. There's more than enough to do to keep you too busy to make money, if you're not careful.

If you can, charge an hourly rate that will make you a living on what you think is a low percentage of billable hours. That way you'll be able to get by until you reach that point, and hours that you work over that percentage will be gravy.

On the other hand, if that hourly rate puts you into a stratospheric fee range, you'll have to do one of three things: 1) find clients willing to pay those rates, 2) increase the number of hours a week you spend looking for clients, or 3) change your target client to one who will give you a higher percentage of billable hours.

Your percentage of billable hours will go up over time. Whether it ever reaches a point where you'll be making money more often than not depends upon your business, clientele, and marketing skills. I have never been satisfied with the number of billable hours I've been able to land, so I've branched my work out into other areas that are more profitable.

If you provide a variety of services, consider charging different rates for each one. There's no reason why your time should be valued at a flat rate across the board. If you've been billing forty and come up with a new service for which the market will bear seventy-five, then split your rates. Just be ready with this as your answer when a client calls, furious because he heard from another client that he's being charged too much. He probably will not have heard that his work is a different service which will cost more, so cool him down and let him know.

A final word about prices. You'll get a feeling for how much is too much. Some of you will discover it earlier than others, which is why I'm hoping that this discussion will open your eyes about what you'll need to bill. Some of you will overvalue yourselves, in which case good luck finding people who will equally overvalue you.

For the rest of you, you'll feel a certain pang when you think about quoting a price that's higher than what you internally think you're worth. This pang will make you say sixty when you were thinking seventy-five, or thirty when you were planning forty. Listen to this inner voice. Once you start charging more than you think you're worth, it will show up negatively in your confidence and in your work. Over time, the amount you're willing to charge will naturally rise—flow with it, don't force it.

Billing by the Hour or by the Project

Service businesses have two primary means of servicing clients. The first is to bill clients by the hour. Typically, the client and the consultant discuss what is to be done, the consultant quotes a range of hours that he estimates the project will take, and the consultant sets off to work. Under this arrangement, the client would normally receive periodic bills from the entrepreneur itemizing the specific work done, the amount of time each task required, and a fee for each task.

The other common method is to quote a set project cost for the entire job. A project cost is a flat fee that stays the same no matter how many hours the project requires. A flat-fee project is usually partially paid in advance, with the remainder due upon completion.

Many clients prefer a flat fee rather than an hourly cost, since it allows them to budget their money more exactly. From the client's point of view, it can be difficult to give a consultant carte blanche to run up charges—they want to know how much they're going to pay, period. Even if they end up paying more for the project than they would have paid by the hour, the certainty of knowing the price makes up for the added cost.

For the entrepreneur, fixed-cost contracts can be a gamble, especially when you're just starting out and aren't sure how long a project will take. If you can finish the work more quickly than you expected, you can pocket the difference. On the other hand, every project has the potential to take more time than you think it will.

I've been burnt twice by flat-fee projects. Once, a database-building project turned out to take four times longer than I'd expected. I later learned that my price had been too low, even for the one-week project I'd anticipated. Colleagues estimated that the work I had done was worth ten times the amount I billed. Live and learn. The second time, a miscommunication between me and my client resulted in her believing that I would do about ten times the work for which I had been contracted. Neither one of these jobs would have been problems on an hourly scale—but at flat fees they became nightmares.

The result is that I am very leery of quoting a flat fee for any consulting work that would naturally be done hourly—training and evaluation chief among them. On the other hand, I have developed specific services that I bill at flat fees, since I approach prospective clients with the project idea and must be able to tell them exactly what it will cost. Since these services vary only in detail, not in scope, I am able to quote a price and not worry about how long the project will take. It gets faster and easier every time I repeat it for a new client.

If a client presses you for a flat fee for hourly services, do the following before you quote a price. Estimate how much time it will take to complete the project. Double it. Multiply by your hourly rate. Then negotiate with the client the scope of the project from beginning to middle to end. Every time he mentions another aspect of the project that you hadn't considered, add doubled time and money to your estimate.

Every time he suggests that he won't need a service that you thought you'd provide, subtract single time and money.

Until you have on paper a shared plan for what the project will be, do not talk fees. Don't suggest a range, don't mention anything other than your normal hourly rate. When you have your complete notes on the estimated project time in front of you, add an additional 25 percent to your fee based on the doubled-time estimates. Then quote that to the client.

Sounds like you're rooking the client out of a lot of money, doesn't it? Not at all—you're covering your behind.

There's no guarantee that your client will take your first offer. The extra 25 percent gives you negotiation room. You can go between that amount and your original doubled-time estimate and still come out ahead.

But whatever you do, don't go below your doubled-time estimate. The reason: fixed-cost projects tend to *at least* double in length. Once the contract is signed, a single call from the client, changing a single parameter, can add ten hours to your work. Sometimes you can charge more money—especially when the new item is not included in the written contract. But if the change is within the bounds of the project, you're out more time. If you don't anticipate this possibility, you're going to end up working for free.

Getting Your Money's Worth in Products

Product-based entrepreneurs should go through the same process as those who are service-based. The difference is in dividing the amount of money you want to make as a salary by the amount of products sold, not by the number of hours worked.

The first step is to determine what each product costs you. That will include the direct cost of all the materials that go into the product, plus a percentage of the indirect costs. Don't forget to build in all indirect costs—a fraction of a cent of each item should reimburse you for that staple gun you had to buy.

Remember also to set aside money for the most important employee, you. The dumb entrepreneur assumes he will live off the profits. The smart one writes a salary into his costs and lets the profits be an added bonus, or earmarks them for expansion of the business.

The difference between direct and fixed (or indirect) costs becomes very clear when you make changes to the business. These changes will affect your bottom line, as the following example illustrates.

Joe's Widget Hut sells about 750 widgets a week, or 39,000 widgets a year. The materials to make each widget cost $1.30. Joe's rent is $500 a month, or $125 a week. Utilities add another $25 a week. Joe's other business-related costs come out to about $2,000 a year, so he factors in $40 a week to cover that amount. He's decided to pay himself $600 for what's usually a sixty-hour workweek.

As a result, Joe's weekly costs are $1,765: (750 widgets × $1.30) + $125 + $25 + $40 + $600. Divide that by 750, and each widget costs him $2.353. Note that I included the tenths-of-a-cent in the calculation—if Joe ignored that, he would be down $117 a year later.

Joe can sell his widgets for $2.36 and still make his salary, but the business won't make any profits. This will cause serious problems down the line if there's a weekly widget slump. Joe has to make his 750 widgets in advance, so if there's a week when he sells only 250, he'll still spend $1,765 that week, but he'll bring in only $590. Unless he has an extra couple thou lying in his bank account, a few weeks like that will put him out of business.

Charging more money will give him more leeway for a bad week. His price should be somewhere in the competitive range, leaning toward the "what the market will bear" standard. One option is to gradually change prices and keep close track of product sales. Another is to charge high prices for most items but always put some products "on sale." The sales will keep the store competitive while the rest of the inventory moves at the best possible price.

After trying out a few different options, Joe decides on a price of $3.50 a widget. This is a markup, or an increase from cost, of about 50 percent. During a good sales week, when he meets his quota of 750, he makes $2,625—which comes to $1,765 in costs (including $600 for his salary), and $860 profit. Some entrepreneurs dip into profits as a second salary—but the smarter thing to do is save it for future business needs and rainy days.

When Joe starts moving more inventory, his business becomes more profitable. If he increases his widget volume to 1,250 a week, his weekly costs go up to $2,415: (1,250 widgets × $1.30) + $125 + $25 + $40 + $600. But his cost per widget goes down to $1.932: $2,415 ÷ 1,250. If he pockets the difference in cost rather than lower his prices, he'll make an additional $315.75 a week on his original volume, plus his profits on the additional 500 widgets.

Generalizing from the widget example, use this as your pricing process:

- Determine your costs, keeping track of those that are fixed and those that vary.

- Add in a salary for yourself that must be paid before the business makes a profit.
- Divide by your sales to determine the base cost per item.
- Add a markup for business profits.
- Check to see if your price is competitive. If it's too low, consider strategies that will reveal what the market will bear for your item. Creative marketing ideas, like those found in chapter 9, can be used to help set your price.

There are many things that can go wrong when you're moving products. Joe's example assumed that he made exactly the right number of widgets every week. In reality, there will be many weeks when Joe has more widgets on hand than he sells; their individual cost to him is still low, but it's money that's tied up in inventory. Until he sells them, he can't spend money on new things. His direct costs will be low until he sells his old widgets, but his fixed costs—rent, utilities, etc.—keep rolling along.

The salary-plus-profit doubled income is meant to act as a hedge against bad times. In many cases, the difference between money that's yours and money that belongs to the business is just an accounting distinction. During bad times, you might have to give some of "your" money back to yourself to keep things going.

Getting Your Money's Worth, Six Months Later

Setting your prices the first time is only half the battle. Eventually, you'll want to increase your profits, as your expertise or product line becomes more valuable. You have two options: sell more product or charge more money. Ultimately, doing both is the way to develop a successful business—but raising prices is easier for the new entrepreneur to handle.

In either products or services, the trick is to bring in more money without cheating existing customers and scaring off new ones. In my business, I have a simple rule: existing clients pay me the same rate they paid on the first day I billed them. Other than that, I change my rates as often as I feel like it.

I feel a certain loyalty to my clients, especially the ones who helped me along when I was just getting off the ground. My hourly rate is now three times what it was when I started. Originally, it was $25, but then I raised it to $40, $60, and $75. There was no particular reason each time I raised it—aside from not being satisfied with my salary, or feeling that my time was being undervalued. At the same time, though, since I have been somewhat capricious about raising my rates, I felt unjustified in hiking up what I charged my existing clients. As I knew it would, it's put me in a position now where several clients can take a whole day from me for relatively little money—so perhaps it would have been smarter to let them know about my tiered system and to promise them a tier lower than my going rate. Since they've already survived several hikes, it will be very difficult to change their rates without a very good reason.

I should point out that the work I am doing now is more specialized—and, to some extent, more skilled—than when I started. I have more experience, more self-confidence, and I'm faster and better at what I do. I've also moved into areas of consulting in which the going rate is double what I charge. So while it's true that I charge some new clients more for what I was doing three years ago, I'm not yet maxing out at what the market will bear. At $75 an hour, I hit my internal "eep!" It didn't feel right to ask for $100. Maybe it will a year from now, or on the day this book is published. I'm just going to listen to myself as best I can, and follow my instincts.

As an entrepreneur, if you're not satisfied with the money you're making, just make more. Don't worry about price resistance until you actually run into some—and then let the quality of your products and services do the convincing.

CHAPTER 6

The Plan

*U*p until now, we've been dealing mostly with safe topics. Entrepreneurs and untrepreneurs would have been equally comfortable with the first few chapters, since they were largely mental exercises. At this point you should have a good image of what your business might be, but it's all in your head so far.

Here's where it gets a little rougher. We're going to start thinking about whys and wherefores, and you're going to need to consider things that are, I guarantee you, totally alien to you. The big-picture types will feel inundated with details, and the bean counters will have to deal with the vision thing.

You're going to need help. Serious help.

A while back I told you not to go shooting your mouth off to your friends, relatives, or nearby homeless people. Now I'm changing that advice. This is when you need to start calling in some big guns: people who know you and can keep you from doing yourself serious damage. Or strangers who have done what you're thinking about doing. Or even professionals who will charge you a couple hundred bucks to answer a few questions.

This is the point when you start seriously investing yourself in your business. I recommend using this time in your development to open yourself up to criticism. Talk to people who might not like your idea. Bounce thoughts off friends who are willing to take you down a peg or two. Put your self-esteem at risk a little, and see if you can take some heat.

When I was at this stage myself, at about t-minus-four-months before I moved and started a new business, I was talking to a friend of mine and asked him what he thought of my idea. His exact words: "I'm worried about you, buddy." He then reminded me about my unfinished grad degrees, my tendency to be scatterbrained, and a few other lunatic ideas that I'd had over the years that never seemed to go anywhere. To him, starting a business seemed like one more half-brained thing that I was trying to pull off, and he had doubts I could do it.

Truth to tell, so did I. And if I hadn't shot my mouth off, or gotten my friends and family invested in my business, I would have probably given up during the worst parts of that half-assed first year. But, for me, the drive to succeed and the fear of having to admit to my friends that, yes, it was a bad idea, kept me going.

Internet

Again, an excellent place to get feedback is from other entrepreneurs on the Internet. Check out the discussions and ask a few questions on misc.entrepreneurs.moderated.

At that point, I owned my business. I had put too much of myself into it to turn back, and that gave me the willpower to hack it.

You can go through the processes in this chapter on your own, and keep everything safe and quiet. But if you've never done this before, it's certain that you're going to get something wrong about what you'll need to do, or about yourself. Bring in your friends and family, talk to trusted mentors, and use everyone around you as a resource to get you through this.

We'll begin laying the groundwork for your business by hammering out a series of details. The best way to work through these details is by writing a business plan.

Business Plans: The Most Useless and Vital Tool You Can Have

That's not a typo. Business plans are frequently the most worthless wastes of time an entrepreneur can go through. They are also absolutely essential to the success of a business. The reason behind this paradox can be found in the variety of business plans that it's possible to write.

In broad terms, a business plan is a blueprint for starting a business. It contains information about the products and services that will be provided, the market, the location of the business, the competition in the area, and projections about how much money the business will need to be started and how much it will make over time. It is meant to encompass the big picture, as well as some of the smaller details.

The secret to writing an effective business plan is knowing the kind you need. In my experience, there are four types:

- *Personal Plan.* This business plan is solely for the use of the entrepreneur, helping her lay out the details of starting a business in an orderly fashion and highlighting those areas that need more work or that have not yet been thought through. It's frequently unpolished and may be written in a shorthand that only the entrepreneur herself can understand, but that's perfectly fine since it is for an intended audience of one.

- *Sounding-Board Plan.* A sounding-board plan is a draft that the entrepreneur shares with friends and respected colleagues. The presentation may be rough, but most of the ideas are in full sentences. Sounding-board plans are written partly to seek new insights into the business, but are also fudged a little to win the approval of the people reading the plan.

- *Seal-of-Approval Plan.* These are given to parents, academic advisors, and spouses to prove that the entrepreneur isn't firmly out of her mind. The plan looks very important and contains pages of charts and figures proving that, after a brief period of time (during which the entrepreneur will be supported by those reading the plan, most likely), there's no question that the new business will be listed in the Fortune 500. The readers of these plans are frequently not businesspeople, so the plans are not airtight and the fudge factor is very high.

- *Formal Plan.* These are the ones mentioned in just about every business book, the ones that get presented

to banks and investors in a quest for money. These follow a rigid structure and have the highest number of
charts, graphs, and figures. They are usually written in
horribly turgid prose, in a vain attempt to disguise
loose ends, and incomplete research.

Some of these are a total waste of time. But one or two of
them will be absolutely necessary for you—which one will depend entirely on your situation. Many entrepreneurs, following the advice in a book, mistakenly sit down to write a
formal business plan, which takes up weeks of their time,
thinking that it's a required step in starting a business. What
they end up with is a plan that most likely is not good
enough to suit any formal purpose. Worse still, they've spent
so much time fitting everything into its proper place that
they don't realize that what they have in their hands is a useless work of fiction.

I spent about three weeks writing my plan of action,
which was a seal-of-approval plan for my parents. They
hadn't asked me for one, but Jewish guilt being what it is, I
went ahead and wrote it anyway. When I was done, I could
show my parents the requisite spreadsheet detailing the
number of clients I would have from month to month; the
income from my fallback work of renting myself and my laptop computer as a secretarial temp, which I projected as my
bread-and-butter income for a few months; the low, middle,
and high estimates of my income for the first three years,
broken down monthly and quarterly; and even documentation showing that I would capture a certain percentage of
Macintosh-consultant market share in the Washington met-
ropolitan area.

I might as well have proven that by 1996 I would be
elected the Queen of Sheba. The whole thing was used a

grand total of once, when I showed it to my parents and some friends and watched their heads nod. My father, who has run a half-dozen businesses, probably knew that he was looking at total garbage, but he was kind enough not to tell me.

The inevitable result was that my life had absolutely nothing to do with the numbers I'd put down on that paper. I vaguely recall rereading it once after moving to Washington, but I'm not certain that I even kept a copy.

So, useless, right? No . . . this was one of the vital plans. The numbers that went into it were fairly worthless, but the process I went through was exactly what I needed at the time. It showed me the areas that I hadn't considered, and started me thinking about things like fallback options and other sources of revenue.

Most importantly, it did two things for my self-esteem: it got me the approval I needed from my parents and the few friends to whom I showed it, and it made me feel, for the first time, like I really had a firm grasp on what I was doing. As it turned out, I was actually fairly clueless, but without the illusion of control, I might not have started in the first place.

The choice of which style to use should be based on what you believe will create the best reference for your future work. Obviously, the more formally you write the plan, the easier it will be to adapt if you need to show it around later to potential sources of money and resources. As we'll discuss in greater detail in chapter 7, a professional presentation of anything you do is crucial to being received with respect and having your ideas heard.

But don't allow the writing of a business plan to become a major sinkhole of your time and effort. There are thousands of untrepreneurs who have business plans for several ideas they've had over the decades, all rotting away on the back shelves of their offices. They took the initial energy and creativity from their business ideas and invested all of it into writing a plan—when they were finished, there was nothing left.

I would recommend that you choose the most rigorous business-plan style that you feel you can tackle responsibly. If all that is, for now, is the personal plan for your own use, then that can be good enough. Remember, though, you might need to do a second plan sometime down the line as you find yourself hemmed in by the vagueness of a personal plan. If you're going to be looking for loans to start a business, you're locked into writing a formal plan eventually. But you can start with one of the others, to give yourself nurturance if that's what you need to accurately understand the components of your business.

Don't Let It Scare You

Many people are very intimidated by the act of setting their ideas on paper. You get two lines into the introductory paragraph, and a small voice in the back of your head says, "This is what I'll be doing for the next God-knows-how-many years? How can I possibly get it right? I have no idea what to put down!"

Now, that small voice has gotten you into a lot of trouble before. This time, though, it's fundamentally correct. It's axiomatic that when you sit down to write a plan for your first business, there's a high probability that you won't know what you're doing. Don't let it bother you.

First off, this is going to be a work of fiction. There are no two ways around that—you're writing about a business that doesn't exist. In my case, I was also writing to some extent about an industry that didn't yet exist: Internet training.

A business plan is inevitably filled with best-guesses, and the whole thing may look pretty flimsy to you when you're done. That's all right, so long as you have some confidence in the process that led you to those guesses.

Second, this does not have to be a document that you write once and finish as though you're turning it in for a grade. It was in my case, and that was a serious mistake. You'll be much better off treating it as a first draft of a work that will never be finished so long as the business is operating. If your plan has some errors or completely off-the-wall mistakes, then you can go back and revise those sections in a few months when you know better.

One of the things on my "to do" list is to take the hundreds of scraps of notes that I have written to help me understand the future of my business, and collate them all into a new business plan, which I can refer to and revise over time. I would have been much better off if this had been my intention from the beginning, starting with my original plan. This would have given me a head start in my work right now, and it would have created a very useful history of my business which, to my regret, now doesn't exist.

Whatever you do, choose a plan and get something written down. It's impossible to keep everything in your head—and the more you write, the more likely your chances of success.

Reading, 'Riting, and 'Rithmetic

The three Rs are the three major components of writing a business plan. You have to do research to determine the nature of your business and the best methods of making it successful. You have to write a narrative explaining your business. And you have to generate some numbers to show

how much money you're going to need while it's gearing up and what you can expect to make from the venture.

All of this is done in a recursive process, meaning that you'll write a section of the plan, and then go back and double-check what you've previously come up with to make certain that everything fits together. For example, when you're generating numbers, you may find that a particular part of your business will cost a lot of money and not turn any profits for you, in which case the smart thing to do is eliminate that part of your idea from the business plan and replace it with something more lucrative.

It's easy at this point to deliberately pull the wool over your own eyes in the hope of making your business seem like a better idea than it actually is, especially if you're doing all this with very little feedback from friends and mentors. Needless to say, this is about the most self-destructive thing you can do right now. If the numbers don't work out right, or if there's some problem that you can't feasibly solve—or even if something just doesn't feel right to you—your best bet is to scrap parts of the plan or even the whole business rather than attempt to stick it out and risk failure. Working out problems will be easier on paper than in real life. If things don't come together in the abstract, you're setting yourself up for a world of hurt.

Research—Hitting the Books and Asking the Experts

Good research is the key to understanding your business and the environment in which you will be working. Optimally, you'll already be familiar with the industry your business is in. The more you know, the better your guesses will be and the more effectively you'll be able to plan.

Research will be an ongoing process throughout the life of your business, but it will be most intensive during the start-up phase. Each component of your business plan will probably require a trip to the library or a series of phone calls. Before we get to that, though, try to understand as holistically as possible your business and the ways in which it will interact with the world. You need to undertake a total immersion, which will leave you with a firmer understanding of how to conduct business and how the particulars of your business will be affected by people, the economy, and political systems around you. This may seem like a tall order, but it's necessary in a world where a government shutdown in Washington can affect salaries in Cairo, and where a factory in Pakistan can cause layoffs in Detroit. Some events might not affect your business directly but will still interfere with or aid your success. Anything that might impact your customer's incomes or the costs of the materials you need will ultimately affect you.

How should you go about this research? There's no end to the number of ways you can add bits of information to your repertoire. Start by using the resources listed below, and remember to cast your net wide. Events and activities that seem peripheral to what you're planning now may very well be central to where you are six months from now. Keep an open mind about how you'll evolve your business, and allow your research to guide you. This is an excellent opportunity to unleash a wellspring of creative ideas for your business and your life.

- *Print Media.* If you don't read a newspaper daily, start. If you do, buy two different dailies. Quality newspapers give a much richer description of the world around you than anything you can find on television. Stay away from *USA Today*, which will give you tons of factoids for your seal-of-approval plan but very little of actual use. If your area doesn't publish a newspaper worth reading, find a newsstand that will sell you the major paper in your region, such as the *New York Times*, the *Los Angeles Times*, or the *Toronto Globe and Mail*. The *Wall Street Journal* can be useful too, but the majority of ink there is geared toward high-finance businesses. I've always thought of it as a great second daily paper, but not good as a primary source.

- *Television and Radio.* I'm addicted to public broadcasting. Thanks to a headset that makes me look like a dorky Martian, I sometimes catch as many as ten hours a day of talk and news. At least once a day there's something on that at least indirectly affects my business. Get into the habit of listening to National Public Radio or the Canadian Broadcasting Company as you commute, clean, or do anything else that leaves your brain in neutral. Get into the habit of scanning the television listings for informative shows that cover your business areas.

- *Libraries and Bookstores.* Pound for pound, books are the most economical way to load your brain with useful information. (And I'm not just saying that because I'm writing this one.) Find a pertinent one, and you'll learn in a day what might take you months to piece together from other sources. Start haunting local public and college libraries. (Most private libraries will allow you to use their facilities but will not give you checkout privileges. Can't hurt to ask.) And while you're at it. . . .

- _Talk to Librarians._ Librarians are one of the best kept secrets of the information age. Sure, that gray-haired man sitting behind the desk might look like he's waiting for you to talk too loud so he can whack you with a ruler—but many of those ruler-wielding silence police got there by virtue of years of study of library science. They know a lot more than you do about where to find information about virtually anything. Cultivate them as a resource, and remember to whisper.

- _Find Future Customers._ If you have any idea who you'll be taking your money from, start tracking them down and asking them questions. Find out what they're looking for in products and services, and get a feel for what they would be willing to pay. Ask them specific questions about aspects of your business plan that are still hazy to you. And offer them a discount or a special service in return for their time. (Suggestions on developing client and prospect questionnaires can be found in chapter 11.)

- _Interview Your Suppliers._ "Supplier" is the usual term for anyone who sells you something you need to do business. This could be the mold for your widget, the Red Dye No. 2 you use for coloring, the cardboard packaging, and the paper you use to write invoices. All businesses, including the purely service-oriented, are dependent on at least some suppliers. Suppliers have been studying your industry for years to better sell you what you need, so feel free to tap them for their help. Find someone who is easy to talk to, and can give you good information—and then repay her by becoming a customer.

- *Professional Help.* At some point along the line, you'll probably need legal and professional help. Why not now? See if you can find a lawyer or accountant who will spare you a half hour off the clock for a debriefing session. Your best bet is to find someone who's self-employed in a small office operation. They'll know that a little time now might make you a client in the future, and you'll get some invaluable information in the process.

- *Potential Future Employees.* If you've already got someone in mind as an employee, take him to lunch and grill him. Give him some ideas about what the business will be. (But not all of the details—some things are better left confidential until you have a better feel for your business. Key among these are financial information and anything else that might give him a leg up in negotiation.) Ask him his opinions, and see what comes out. Not only will you get a handle on whether this person would be a good fit for your business, but you might also land some valuable ideas and someone to run with them in the bargain.

- *Small Business Development Centers.* SBDCs are organizations sponsored by business schools and businesses in the area. They provide a variety of resources to entrepreneurs. Most require a business plan before they'll give you one-on-one support, but their resources can be useful in the preparation of the plan.

  You can find an SBDC by calling the Small Business Administration (listed below), or checking a phone book or local library.

- *Uncle Sam.* Your tax dollars at work, no sarcasm intended. The Small Business Administration provides a range of valuable services to entrepreneurs starting and expanding their businesses, and will continue to do so unless the Republicans shut them down. Catch up with them by calling (800) 368-5855. The SBA also can refer you to services run by other agencies that may be germane to your business, such as the Service Corps of Retired Executives (SCORE). Be sure to ask who else you should call.

- *Approach the Competition.* Yeah, I know, it sounds nuts. You're about to try to take his business away, so why would he talk to you? It depends on the situation and how you broach the topic.

Internet

You just started a business? What are you going to do next? The correct answer is, "I'm going to FedWorld!" FedWorld isn't an amusement park for FBI agents, but the granddaddy of all government Web sites. Chalk one up to the bureaucrats—they did this one right. Just about anything that the government provides for free in computer format can be found here.

Business resources change all the time, but a sampling of what's here includes the Consumer Information Center (those people in Pueblo, Colorado, who have been telling you about their catalog all these years); the Census, which has plenty of demographic information over and above a simple head count; the Department of Commerce; and the Small Business Administration. The SBA's Web page gets you right to the heart of it with categories on starting, financing, and expanding your business.

It's worth noting that FedWorld was available (at http://www.fedworld.gov.) even when the federal government was shut down, making it the fastest way to find useful government information.

There are probably businesses in your area that parallel what you're planning to do, but that aren't in direct competition. In my case, I learned a lot from an IBM consultant (such as why anyone would want to go near Windows), and since all of my clients are Mac-based, he had nothing to lose. He may even gain some business, since I'll refer IBM clients his way if they contact me about services.

Or maybe you'll find direct competitors that won't see you as a threat. I'm always willing to talk shop with competitors—the market's wide enough that I doubt any one of them could take enough business away from me to hurt me. If I make sure that I get as much good information as I give, I come out ahead. (People who don't know when to shut up always lose in these situations.)

Internet

All of these resources are easily available in online communities. You'll be able to quickly identify numerous people who may be able to help you—just be sure to communicate with them first and build up a rapport before you try to pick their brains. A major advantage to online support is getting your responses by e-mail; a written answer will almost always be more thoughtful and useful than an off-the-cuff spoken reply.

Another major advantage is diversity. Unless you really go out of your way, I'm willing to wager that most of your sources will be a fairly homogenous group: all local, all of one gender, or all of a similar age. The Internet opens you up to international perspectives, which can go a long way toward throwing a crowbar into a closed mind and letting the air in.

Some people resort to subterfuge—calling a competitor and posing as a client to get pricing information. This is a common occurrence, and many entrepreneurs develop sensitive antennae that quiver when they are being scammed. I don't recommend it, but sometimes it's the only way to go. Just don't complain later when someone does the same thing to you.

All that should give you plenty of places to start looking for help and information. If you go to the well and it turns up dry—and no one knows anything about your planned business—you'll be in one of two situations. The business might be such a bad idea that no one has ever been able to make it viable, and so there are no such businesses. Or you may be the first person to stumble upon a Holy Grail, wide-open business niche, which is yours to exploit to the fullest until someone else sees you doing it.

The only way to figure that one out is more research.

Components of the Business Plan

Time to kill two birds with one stone. As we go over each part of the business plan, we'll also discuss the factors involved in making the necessary decisions. There's no point in writing a business plan flying blind, so this will get yours written and a bunch of decisions made at the same time.

Again, I remind you that you're not writing the Dead Sea Scrolls here. If you come across something that confuses you, or you feel like what you're writing wouldn't have gotten you through the easiest pass-fail course you ever took, do the best you can, make a note of it, and come back to it later.

Don't agonize—but try not to skip anything. Glossing over a particular section may indicate that you need to work harder on that area. A vague description will give you more to work with than nothing at all—gaping holes play hell with building coherent overviews.

If you're writing a formal business plan, you'll find a rigorous outline for one later in this chapter. None of the other types of plans need to be as regimented so long as all of the key questions are answered. No matter what type of plan you write, be certain to keep your audience in mind and to write appropriately for them.

The Executive Summary

Every business plan should lead off with a one-page description of the business and a summary of important details from the rest of the plan. This is important when you show the plan to anyone else, since chances are they won't give the entire thing a rigorous read. In many formal plans, this is the only part that is guaranteed to get read at all, so draw them in with the summary or lose the potential funder.

Even if you're the only person you ever expect to read this, write a summary anyway. If you can't describe your business in two sentences, you won't be able to sell the concept to clients, customers, and business contacts. Complex ideas must be made clear, and everything must be concise.

You'll hit your first roadblock on the third or fourth word, when you realize that you're writing about a business that hasn't been *named* yet. The name of a business is very important to setting the standards by which it is judged. My business, Millennium Consulting, attracts a different kind of clientele than Porten's PC Problem-Solving would. Some things to consider:

- *The Name Should Reflect the Spirit of the Business.* Cutesy names that rhyme or play on words can work wonders in a business where wit is appreciated. But you'll notice that no doctor's office is named "Cures For What Ails Ya!" The tone of your name will affect how people judge your professionalism. Creativity-based and product-based businesses are far more likely to benefit from cute names than service businesses. Ask potential customers and others for their take on your name. If it's unoriginal or—even worse—offensive or juvenile, you'll shoot yourself in the foot.

- *Don't Constrain Yourself.* One of the most popular video-game systems in my day was the ColecoVision. For the 80s, this was a cool-sounding name that played on Coleco, the name of the company. Then I found out it had originally been named the Connecticut Leather Company. No one in their right mind would buy a video game from a company with a name like *that.* Name changes can be expensive and time-consuming, so start with one that covers other areas into which you might expand. Millennium Consulting is perfect for this, implying a high-tech air but at the same time not saying anything specific about what I do. That flexibility has often been useful.

- *No One Is Fooled by the Appearance of Numbers.* I've seen a number of businesses called The Smith Group, or something similar. Invariably, the group is a single person who mistakenly believes he'll have more clout if he seems like more people. It's all right to use the pronoun "we" when "I" is more accurate, but don't push this by adding it to your name. You'll look foolish to clients who realize you're the only person answering the phone.

- *Including Your Name Might Save Some Hassle.* The classic entrepreneurial ego trip is to use your last name in the title. This won't do you much good until people start to know your name, but one area where it will provide some leverage is in legal registration, since using your real name may reduce paperwork and fees.

Now that that's done, the rest of the executive summary should seem easier. There are two ways to go about writing this part: doing it immediately, or doing it last, after the rest of the plan is completed. I recommend the former. It will certainly require several rewrites, but it will also show you which elements you are inclined to miss the first time around, which will be valuable information about your working process.

Goals and Mission

What is the overall aim of your company? "Making money" is not good enough. Your company should have a clearly stated purpose, such as "Millennium Consulting will provide exemplary Macintosh training and World Wide Web publishing services to small businesses, primarily those located in the Washington area."

Elaborate on the mission by explaining briefly how your company will strive for these goals: "Millennium will offer a mix of personalized training, seminars, and publications that will teach its clients to be power-users of their equipment. Millennium will provide everything they need to know, and not bog them down in extraneous technological details."

It should go without saying, but be certain that your company's mission dovetails with the personal mission that you developed a few chapters ago. If spending time with your family is a key life goal, don't generate a mission that will force you to go on the road three hundred days a year. Many entrepreneurs follow the smell of money and end up as trapped in their own businesses as they were in their jobs. A strong mission statement that keys into your values is some protection against that occurring.

The Players

Who will be the people working in this business? At the very least, there will be one employee: you. Include a full résumé of your past experiences and skills. Again, even if you are your own audience, the process of going through your background will help you recognize the talents that will serve your business best.

Anyone else? That will depend on what you'll be selling. Many businesses are absolutely dependent on a team of employees; others get by perfectly well with just the entrepreneur running the show.

Employees infinitely increase the stress and complexity of running a business. From the start, they require much more paperwork and record-keeping to ensure that you're following all pertinent employment laws. (Since you won't know what's pertinent in your area, expect to run up some attorney fees.) And since most employees feel it's pretty important to get paid, you're setting yourself up for a major recurring expense. On the other hand, tons of businesses simply *must* have employees. You won't be able to offer twenty-four-hour services, or handle a high sales volume, all on your own. If your business isn't clearly a one-person or a staffed operation, try thinking in terms of your skills and talents. Do you have the repertoire necessary to handle all the tasks of the business on your own? Employees are an excellent way to fill in weak spots, and they make impossible tasks merely Herculean by dividing and conquering the work.

Since employees cost a lot of money, keep your need for them to a bare minimum and to yourself alone if at all possible. However, if you know you will need some employees from the beginning, include as much information about them as possible in the business plan—specific names and résumés if you already have them chosen, job descriptions and desired personality types if not.

If you're writing a seal-of-approval or formal business plan, include information here about professionals whose services you will use—lawyers, accountants, and consultants. You don't need to retain their services at this point, but you'll want to at least have names to turn to when the time comes. This is useful for any type of plan, but is especially necessary for the more rigorous varieties to demonstrate no stone left unturned.

Lastly, if you're writing a business plan for the express intent of getting funding from investors, make sure that your team includes someone experienced with the ways of business. Investors are more interested in your track record than in your killer business idea, and it's a sure bet that your record won't be particularly impressive unless you made a few million cornering the bubble-gum market in elementary school. Adding some "gray hair"—in the form of an experienced businessperson who can come on board as a consultant, member of a board of advisors, or even as staff—will go a long way toward soothing nervous investors and opening wallets. If you don't know anyone appropriate, contact SCORE—call the SBA at (800) 368-5855 to find the office nearest you.

Product and Services Description

Describe the products and services that your business will provide. Go into as much detail as possible, and list any ancillary revenues that you can generate. For example, your primary business might be selling widgets, but you might also offer a training service demonstrating how to use the widget effectively. Go into serious hype mode here—you want your readers to come away utterly convinced that your business is providing a necessary service. List the factors that make your products and services more attractive than what is currently available, and the reasons why your team is expert in making products, providing services, and selling them to your market.

Market Overview

What is the environment in which your business will operate? What impact will other businesses have on the way you conduct your own? Who are the people you will be trying to reach, and why will they be interested in buying your offerings? (Don't worry yet about *how* you'll reach them; that's later.)

This section may require some serious legwork. You've heard about focus groups being used to test everything from toothpaste to presidential candidates. Those are the same questions you'll have to ask to know what you're talking about in your market overview. Run through the list of suggested research resources that I listed above, and track down everything you can about your market. This is one area in which you can't know too much, even if not all of it makes it into the plan. (Putting it all into the formal plan is mandatory, though. Your investors will want to know you've done your homework.)

Your research will probably turn up a wide swath of potential customers crossing many demographic categories. It's important to find the proper balance between a large enough market to sustain your business, but not one so large that it dilutes your ability to reach them. As a small business, you won't be able to sell to every fifty-five to sixty-four-year-old in the country; focus on a niche that you'll be able to cover.

Competition

What businesses will you be competing with for your clientele? What are they doing right, and what are they doing wrong? What will be your competitive edge over them, and how will you maintain that edge after they catch on and catch up to you? This is another one that's going to send you back to the books and reference sources.

Many business books tell you to worry about something called market share here. Market share is a percentage of the total business out there—the number of products sold by a specific business, divided by the total number of the same products sold by all businesses. If the entire city of Washington buys a hundred million yards of red tape a year, and 7-Eleven sells fifteen million yards, that's a 15 percent market share.

W hen I started, I had the idea that I would provide consulting services for anyone with a computer—but I quickly changed to targeting Macintosh-based clients. Even so, I mistakenly took on a number of clients who were outside my target market, which invariably took three to four times as much effort as clients with whom I was more surefooted. Dispersing your energies this way is not a good idea—don't make the same mistake.

Market share is vitally important when the total market can sustain only a few businesses, or when the investment in a business is so high that it requires mass consumption to turn a profit. In my experience, for most small businesses market share is a charade. I have a ballpark idea of how many people in Washington use Macintoshes, but I have no clue how many of them are using consultants, or what my market share is. It doesn't matter—there's enough business going around to support both me and my competitors. That answer won't be good enough for a formal plan, but for any other plan, crunching numbers is probably a waste of time.

A problem that turns up more frequently than you might expect is *finding* competitors. After three years, I know only two other people in my area who provide the same service I do, and for some ancillary work I do, so far as I can determine, I have *no* competition. If your idea is truly fresh and creative, you may have difficulty finding someone whose own product overlaps yours enough to call them competition.

But don't think that means the golden road to riches is open to you. Even if no one else sells your service, other people will be marketing items that compete for the same sales that you're competing for. Anyone else with whom they might spend money, for something in a similar category as your own product or service, is your competition. Find out who these people are and write them up in your plan.

Is your competition going to change much in the future? It could if there are low "barriers to entry" in your market. These are conditions that prevent others from doing the work that you are. Chrysler isn't that worried about new competitors because few people have a billion dollars to build a car factory. Unfortunately, the same factors that make businesses attractive to young entrepreneurs—low start-up costs primary among them—make it easy for others to duplicate what you're doing. There are no rewards for being first if someone can quickly do it better. Try to determine if anyone else will try to follow in your footsteps and trample you along the way. Then come up with ways to prevent that. Generating high loyalty among clients and creative marketing are good alternatives to having a hefty bankroll.

Location

The right business location is essential to success—more important than gold for good business health. We'll discuss why in detail in chapter 7. When you've settled on a prime spot, be certain to include information about it and the reasons for it in your business plan.

Marketing

Build a better mousetrap, and the world will channel-surf right past you—unless you can break through their collective, attention-deficient consciousness. This is also too big to tackle here; come back with a detailed marketing summary after you've developed a plan of attack with the help of chapter 9.

Risks and Potential for Error

Now that you've written the plan, what might you have gotten wrong, or miscalculated? Make an honest attempt here to explain the risks of your venture, any research materials that you needed but couldn't find, and other monkey wrenches that were thrown in along the way. Then describe what you're going to do in the event that things go wrong. If there's a single linchpin on which your business hinges, try to come up with some change to the business plan that will make you less vulnerable. Otherwise you're playing Russian roulette.

Crunching Numbers

This is possibly the worst part of starting a business: coming up with detailed numbers that show where the money will be coming from and going to. There are three reasons why writing the required financial information in a business plan is difficult.

First, it's one thing to write a narrative paragraph or two about a business that doesn't yet exist, and quite another to write down that you'll be making exactly x dollars during March of next year. In computers there's an expression for what you're risking here: GIGO, or Garbage In, Garbage Out. If your numbers are based on wrong suppositions and there are errors in your expectations, the results will be totally worthless.

Second, numbers are supposed to be more rigorous. I had a hell of a time doing this part of my business plan because I knew without a doubt that my financials were GIGO. It bothered me, and it made it more difficult to convey my ideas to people who asked me questions about the numbers. That wasn't particularly important in my case, but it would have hurt me if someone was basing whether to lend me money on my financial plans. Even if my numbers had been sound, I had little confidence in them, which can translate to low confidence in the business.

Third, financial planning is essentially writing a budget for yourself and your business. For most of us, starting with no assets and a history of spending every dollar we've made on essentials like food, shelter, and CDs, a budget predicting our financial lives is a new and frightening prospect. Yet that is what's required in a business plan.

There are no easy solutions to these problems. You will have to write your financials in a sound fashion, and that may require additional research into the small details that add up to large costs. ("What's the business registration fee for my part-time distributor in Pensacola?" "What is the tax difference between this side and that side of the county line?") Much of this will require drudgery on your part, but the advantage to it—and the reason why the people with the bucks require it of you—is that it will leave you with an understanding of the realities of your business.

The Pro Forma—
The Devil's in the Details

The financial plan section of your business plan is called the pro forma or, frequently, just the "financials." It is essentially a detailed budget showing how the money will flow through your business, where it will be distributed, and how profitable you will be over the next few years.

You can think of it as a glorified personal budget—which is actually a very good idea if you're starting a business as a sole proprietor. Your business finances *are* your personal finances, so why not make plans for what you'll be spending on keeping yourself alive in the process? This requires, of course, that your business plan is for your use only, or as a sounding board. Formal business plans, and some seal-of-approval plans, won't fly with a line-item expense for Doritos and dip. In those cases, write a personal budget in addition to the pro forma, and make certain that the money coming out of the business will cover your personal needs.

Your first step is to determine what categories of expenses you expect to have in the coming few years. Here's a sample list with my annotations; I grabbed the list of categories as a selection of suggestions in my Quicken personal-finance program.

We'll start with expenses that are primarily personal—although some personal expenses tend to go up when you start a business:

- *Auto.* Think of everything it costs to keep your car in working order. Be sure to budget for gasoline, maintenance, and annual inspections. If the car will be used regularly for the business, expect these costs to be higher in the future than they have been in the past.
- *Bank Charges.* For the most part, small businesses don't run much in the way of bank fees. A sole proprietor can get away with using a personal account, with monthly fees ranging from $15 a month to zero if you

I am deliberately using a canned list from a piece of software to demonstrate one of the subtle advantages of using a computer for your financial planning. Most financial software packages have been around long enough in a competitive environment that they come with some very good tips on writing your own budgets. The multimedia versions will even walk you through the process step by step. This kind of assistance is certainly worth the cost of the software.

maintain a minimum balance. Partnerships and corporations require a separate business account, for which banks charge at least $10 a month while providing fewer services than they do for individuals. Sole proprietors should not allow their banks to change their accounts to business accounts. Instead, find a bank that will set up a personal account that is listed as "trading as" your business name. This will let you deposit checks written to your business without incurring the costs of a business account.

- *Child Care.* Have a kid? Expecting one anytime soon? If you're thinking of having children in the next few years, ask a friend who's already had one how much the little buggers cost. Then add those figures here. (Having a child in the first few years after starting a business is, in my opinion, a grade-A rotten idea. Your stress level will be high enough already, and your time will be owned by the business. Better to wait until you know how your life will go before you add new responsibilities.)

- *Clothing.* If you're the clothes-horse type, tack on a monthly figure that won't make you resort to second-hand stores or (horrors!) wearing clothes that are out of style. If you're like me, though, budgeting for new socks and underwear every six months should do it. Don't forget to include the cost of business clothing if you need monkey suits to greet clients and you don't own any.

- *Education.* Still paying a tuition bill? Have student loans coming up? Need part-time course work to be certified for your business? Write 'em down.

- *Entertainment.* Most of us have no idea how much we shell out for concert tickets and movies. Keep track of what you spend for a while, and then decide to cut down or budget for it.

- *Gifts.* It's the American way to forget about Christmas until November and then run up a credit-card debt. This is merely silly for most people, but for new business owners on tight budgets, it can be suicidal.

- *Groceries.* Same deal as entertainment. Don't make a wild guess here; keep track for a while and then budget it in. And consider buying store brands and saving your nickels.

- *Household.* This includes everything that you blow money on for your home or apartment. It won't add up to much for renters, but it's enough that forgetting it could leave you strapped.

- *Miscellaneous.* It's worth budgeting money here on the assumption that you've forgotten something elsewhere.

- *Recreation.* I'm not sure how the Quicken folks intend this to be different from entertainment, but I would budget money here for vacation costs (not that you should be planning any), health and fitness clubs, bungee jumping, paint-ball gun refills, and anything else you enjoy and want to keep doing.

- *Rent.* This is the big one in most budgets. Incidentally, your rent payment each month isn't supposed to be more than 25 percent of your overall income. If your apartment costs you more than a quarter of what you expect to make for the foreseeable future, move.

- *Restaurants.* This sometimes costs me more than rent. Keep track of what you're spending here, and don't forget to include small snacks and sodas that aren't full meals at restaurants, but cost money regardless. Forgetting 50¢ a day will leave you nearly $200 short after a year.

- *Subscriptions.* This will be an important expense only if you'll need to buy a trade journal to stay on top of your industry. Some of those can cost hundreds of dollars annually.
- *Taxes.* In a formal plan, you'll need to calculate exactly what your taxes will be based on the other numbers in the plan, and budget the payments in the proper months. For other plans, put in a line-item cost of 20 to 30 percent of your income. Businesses must make tax payments quarterly, not annually, so spread those payments out over the year. More information about calculating your taxes can be found in chapter 7.
- *Telephone.* Use the average of your last few bills.
- *Travel.* What will you have to spend to get to and from your clients and prospects? Are there any upcoming family reunions that you cannot escape? Budget these trips now or cancel them later.
- *Utilities.* This includes water and gas, phone bills, electricity, that sort of thing. Expect these to go up if you're working at home during very hot or cold weather.

Now for expenses that are business-specific:

- *Advertising.* Most businesses require some kind of advertising budget—but not all. Figure a few twenties a month for ads in small printed publications, low hundreds for radio, high hundreds for newspapers, and well into the thousands for television. Put down a rough estimate for now, but don't use that for any serious calculations until you've read more about marketing in chapter 9.

- *Bad Debt.* Every business has deadbeats. Some businesses are more prone to them than others. You can take steps to prevent this from happening to you, but for now it would be wise to budget a few percent of your total income lost to bad debt. (I've had slow debt, but no bad debt so far. Knock on wood.)
- *Benefits.* Benefits for employees tend to cost about one-third over and above their salaries, so budget that for your full-timers. Full-time employees cost a lot of money and drastically increase expenses. At this point, most of you without starting funds shouldn't be thinking about paying benefits, but you do need to include the cost of your own benefits!
- *Cost of Goods.* If you're selling a product, you've got to buy it or make it. That runs up two expenses: labor and materials. (You can exclude labor expenses if they're already covered under wages.)
- *Dues.* Any professional organizations that you'll need to join charge membership fees.
- *Entertainment.* Factor in any additional expenses you're expecting from wining and dining your clients. Keep these expenditures separate from your personal entertainment budget, as these are tax-deductible. And keep these as low as possible—high entertainment budgets are a red flag for investors and the tax man alike.
- *Insurance.* You may need to take out policies to cover your business in case of an act of God or, worse still, an act of lawyer. More research is needed for this one— you'll find some pointers in chapter 7.
- *Interest.* Don't forget to factor in any money you'll be paying for business loans or other debts.

- *Janitorial.* It'll cost money to keep your place of business clean—unless you're in a home office, where you can pick up your own laundry.
- *Legal and Professional Fees.* Usually abbreviated L&P fees, these are the hundreds of dollars an hour you'll spend on lawyers, accountants, and consultants. Sole proprietors can budget this at next to nothing, so long as there's money in the miscellaneous fund to cover the unexpected. Partnerships and corporations should expect to watch their money flow out of this pipeline on a regular basis.
- *Rent.* This is rent for your place of business, not personal rent. If your office is the space under your bed or in the broom closet, you can skip this one.
- *Returns.* Factor in the amount you expect to lose when customers come back with your widget and get their money back. Lost money is the same as spent money, so it appears here. This applies only to product-based businesses; it's a lot harder to return advice or consulting work. Five percent of your expected sales should cover you, but increase that if your products don't go through a rigorous quality review.
- *Supplies.* Think of all the supplies that will go into your office or place of business. This could involve thousands of little details, so come up with a ballpark figure, then double it and write it down. Chances are you forgot about half of what you'll need.
- *Taxes.* If you plan to incorporate your business, you'll have to pay taxes separate from those listed on your personal budget.
- *Telephone.* This includes costs for second phone lines, fax lines, and long-distance calls. Add in any high-tech services you'll be getting from your local Baby Bell, such as voice mail, call forwarding, or Caller ID. If you

plan to buy new equipment, such as cordless phones or answering machines, they go here too.

- *Travel.* Estimate any expenses you may need for business trips. The daily commute to and from your main place of business doesn't count. New entrepreneurs should try to keep these very low, but don't be pound foolish by missing important trade shows and conferences.
- *Utilities.* Same as before—water and gas, phone bills, electricity.
- *Wages.* Unless you're a latter-day Svengali, you'll have to pay your employees. I recommend being parsimonious with salaries and generous with profit-linked bonuses and commissions. If you plan to pay your employees this way, break down wages into fixed monthly costs and commission costs.

Enough expenses—they're getting me depressed. Let's talk about income. Income, naturally, comes in far fewer categories:

- *Bonuses.* These are rare for our age group, but if a previous employer owes you money in the form of a bonus, a lump-sum check from her will do nice things for your bottom line that month.
- *Client Fees.* This category accounts for the major source of income for client-based service businesses.
- *Family Support.* If you can nail down Mom and Dad or Uncle Leo to give you some sort of stipend, or even if you just expect that their support will be steady enough that you can gauge it from month to month, there's no reason not to include that in your plans. This should definitely be left out, though, in formal plans and even seal-of-approval plans if you think your

golden goose might see these numbers and get offended enough to cut you off.

- *Gross Sales.* This is the main source of income for product-based businesses. "Gross" doesn't refer to the quality of the goods, but rather is a business term meaning every dime that is raked in, before you subtract the myriad expenses and taxes that keep this from being all yours.
- *Interest Income.* If you've got any money in savings worth noting, or stocks that pay dividends, include that income here. For most of us, this will be about a nickel or so a month, so you can skip it here—but not on your tax forms, where forgetting to pay taxes on 60¢ could run you $30 or $40 in fines two years down the line.
- *Salary.* If you're going to be working for someone else part-time, or even full-time during the very early days of your business, include it here.

Plotting It Out

Now that you have all of your categories, start filling in the blanks. If you're writing this down before you've taken the

Bonuses, family support, and salaries are all forms of personal income. You can include them on pro formas when you combine your personal and business finances to get a more accurate picture of exactly how broke you'll be in the first few months. Leave these out of formal plans, since personal income doesn't count as business income and it will look like you're cooking the books. If you must include your own cash in the first months of a formal business plan, list it as an interest-free loan from yourself, to be paid back by the business in the future.

time to calculate some of these numbers, scribble down a best guess now, but make a note to yourself to come back and fix it later with better numbers. Since each of your expenses will be broken down by month, a mistake of only $10 or $20 can mean hundreds at the end of the year. Repeat this mistake across several categories, and you'll be seriously fubar (an Army term, for—politely—fouled up beyond all recognition).

Your plan has to stretch out monthly for at least twelve months. Monthly expectations beyond that tend to verge from the fictional into the outrageously fanciful. However, when I did my plan, for some reason the end of the year confused the hell out of me. I wasn't sure how to deal with partial-year earnings as a predictor of future business and for tax purposes. In the end, it turned out that it was all rather easy, but if the number crunching confuses you, extend your monthlies out for the remainder of this year, and then all of next year. Your numbers for the end of next year won't be worth much, but at least you'll have a full calendar year in front of you.

Uncle Sam, in his infinite wisdom, allows you to make things even more confusing. You can declare a fiscal year that is different from the calendar year—July through June. For some businesses, this makes a lot of sense as they adjust the timing of their tax payments to reflect seasonal increases in income. If you're a sole proprietor and you're not relying on an accountant, don't even think about doing this. If you've already retained the services of a professional, though, it'll be worth the fifteen minutes of his time to ask him whether you should use calendar or fiscal years.

TABLE 1 Sample Pro Forma

	Jan	Feb	Mar	Apr	May	Jun	Jul	Aug	Sep	Oct	Nov	Dec
Personal Expenses												
Auto	0	0	0	0	0	0	0	0	0	0	0	0
Bank charges	5	5	5	5	5	5	5	5	5	5	5	5
Child care	0	0	0	0	0	0	0	0	0	0	0	0
Clothing	200	20	20	20	20	100	20	20	20	20	20	20
Education	65	65	65	65	65	65	65	65	65	65	65	65
Entertainment	10	10	15	15	20	20	30	30	40	40	50	50
Gifts	0	0	0	0	30	30	0	0	0	0	0	50
Groceries	40	40	40	40	40	40	40	40	40	40	40	40
Household	20	20	20	20	20	20	20	20	20	20	20	20
Miscellaneous	20	20	20	20	20	20	20	20	20	20	20	20
Recreation	0	0	0	0	0	0	0	0	0	0	0	0
Rent	425	425	425	425	425	425	435	435	435	435	435	435
Restaurants	20	20	25	25	30	30	40	40	50	50	60	60
Subscriptions	0	0	0	150	0	0	0	0	0	0	0	0
Taxes	0	0	0	0	0	0	0	0	0	0	0	0
Telephone	50	50	50	60	60	60	70	70	70	80	80	80
Travel	0	0	0	0	100	0	0	0	0	0	0	100
Utilities	0	0	0	0	0	0	0	0	0	0	0	0
Total Personal	$855	$675	$685	$845	$835	$815	$745	$745	$765	$775	$795	$945
Business Expenses												
Advertising	75	75	75	75	75	75	125	125	125	125	125	125
Bad debt	0	12.50	12.50	25	25	30	30	35	35	40	40	45
Benefits	75	75	75	75	75	75	75	75	75	75	75	75
Cost of goods	0	0	0	0	0	0	0	0	0	0	0	0
Dues	0	0	0	0	0	0	0	0	0	0	0	0
Entertainment	20	20	30	30	40	40	40	40	50	50	50	50

	Jan	Feb	Mar	Apr	May	Jun	Jul	Aug	Sep	Oct	Nov	Dec
Insurance	0	0	0	0	0	0	0	0	0	0	0	0
Interest	0	0	0	0	0	0	0	0	0	0	0	0
Janitorial	0	0	0	0	0	0	0	0	0	0	0	0
L & P fees	200	0	0	100	0	0	0	0	0	0	0	100
Rent	0	0	0	0	0	0	0	0	0	0	0	0
Returns	0	0	0	0	0	0	0	0	0	0	0	0
Supplies	50	20	20	20	20	20	20	20	20	20	20	20
Taxes	0	0	0	0	0	0	0	0	0	0	0	0
Telephone	0	0	0	0	0	0	165	15	15	15	15	15
Travel	0	0	0	0	0	300	0	0	0	0	0	0
Utilities	0	0	0	0	0	0	0	0	0	0	0	0
Wages	0	0	0	0	0	0	100	100	100	100	100	100
Total Business	$420	$203	$213	$325	$235	$540	$555	$410	$420	$425	$425	$530
Total Expenses	$1,275	$878	$898	$1,170	$1,070	$1,355	$1,300	$1,155	$1,185	$1,200	$1,220	$1,475
Income												
Bonuses	0	0	0	0	0	0	0	0	0	0	0	0
Client Fees	0	250	250	500	500	600	600	700	700	800	800	800
Family Support	500	500	500	500	500	500	250	250	250	250	250	250
Gross Sales	0	0	0	0	0	0	0	0	0	0	0	0
Interest	.77	2.62	4.21	3.85	3.42	3.25	2.61	1.47	.95	.35	0	0
Salary	1500	750	0	0	0	0	0	0	0	0	0	0
Total Income	$2,001	$1,503	$754	$1,004	$1,003	$1,103	$853	$951	$951	$1,050	$1,050	$1,150
Cash on Hand												
Balance	300	1,026	1,651	1,507	1,341	1,274	1,022	575	371	137	(13)	(183)
Income	2,001	1,503	754	1,004	1,003	1,103	853	951	951	1,050	1,050	1,150
Expenses	1,275	878	898	1,170	1,070	1,355	1,300	1,155	1,185	1,200	1,220	1,475
End of Month	$1,026	$1,651	$1,507	$1,341	$1,274	$1,022	$575	$371	$137	($13)	($183)	($508)

I've written a hypothetical pro forma, which you'll find in table 1. (See table 1, "Sample Pro Forma.") It's written exactly the way I wrote my first pro forma, and in the manner that I expect you to write yours—totally off the top of my head. Brainiacs amongst you will notice the result of this kind of planning, as this particular plan has our fictional entrepreneur bankrupted by the end of the year.

If this happens to you too, don't panic. You're not in the soup line yet. This just demonstrates how difficult it is to write a budget, and how important it is to stick to it. Any variation can leave you on what's left of welfare in your state.

Take a look at the organization of the pro forma. When you write yours, you don't need to include lines that will always be zero—I've just done it here for clarity's sake. Here are some explanations for how I came up with those numbers, which as you'll see are idiosyncratic and will vary based on your business and lifestyle. Personal expenses:

- *Auto.* The best way to save money on your car is not to own one. Public transit is your friend.
- *Bank Charges.* I'm assuming that what our friend saves when his balance is high, he'll end up paying in ATM charges.
- *Child Care.* No kids, which at this point is a good thing.
- *Clothing.* This allows him $200 for a new suit or two to start, then socks and underwear for the year, with a midyear sprucing up in June. When he doesn't blow $20 in any given month, I figure he'll end up needing what he's saved eventually.
- *Education.* Fortunately, he has just one modest student loan payment.
- *Entertainment.* I allowed him only a spartan entertainment budget at first, but gradually increased it so he could have a decent social life.

- *Gifts.* Our hero sets money aside for Mother's Day, Father's Day, and Christmas. It's a good thing his friends don't have birthdays.
- *Groceries and Household.* These numbers work if he clips coupons.
- *Miscellaneous.* A slush fund of $20 a month keeps him from going over budget.
- *Recreation.* Yes, it's possible: a full year with no parties, vacations, or pleasures of the flesh that cost anything.
- *Rent.* I factored in a rent increase halfway through the year. Unless you have very generous landlords, expect your rent to go up, too.
- *Restaurants.* Some people can cut this out entirely, and more power to them. This budget starts out small and then works up to a semi-decent amount of money for eating out.
- *Taxes.* He sets aside $150 to cover anything they forgot to take out for last year.
- *Telephone.* Same as restaurants. He starts with very few calls, but works this number up to where he'd like it to be.
- *Travel.* This will pay for round-trip tickets and other costs for Alumni Day and New Year's trips.
- *Utilities.* I very optimistically assumed that his $425 apartment would include utilities. There's no such place near where I live, but let's say the hypothetical man lives elsewhere.

Business expenses:

- *Advertising.* These numbers allow for a small print ad in a local newspaper at first, increasing in the second half of the year.
- *Bad Debt.* This is set to 5 percent of the client fees for each month.
- *Benefits.* This allows a simple medical insurance plan for the business owner.

- *Cost of Goods.* My hypothetical entrepreneur is in services, not products, so he doesn't have any goods costs.
- *Entertainment.* As he starts moving into high-gear networking, the number of meet-and-greets, lunches, and drinks with the business community goes up.
- *Insurance.* Assuming sole proprietorship and a business that doesn't take extraordinary risks, no additional insurance for the business is needed.
- *L&P Fees.* I factored in $200 for up-front information about starting a business, $100 more at tax time to help take care of last year, and another $100 at the end of the year for general bookkeeping help.
- *Rent.* Our entrepreneur has a home office, so there are no additional rent costs.
- *Supplies.* This simple sole proprietorship needs only $50 to kick off, $20 a month thereafter.
- *Telephone.* These are additional telephone costs incurred solely by the business. I'm assuming no additional costs for six months, then the installation of a second line and monthly costs for that line after that.
- *Travel.* Mr. Hypothetical takes a trip to a trade show in June.
- *Wages.* He had no employees for the first six months, but then hired a college student part-time to help with some of the scut work.

Income:
- *Bonuses.* One big goose egg.
- *Client Fees.* He earns nothing the first month, but his income steadily builds thereafter.
- *Family Support.* Uncle Leo pitches in $500 per month while things are getting started, reducing his support to $250 after six months.

- *Interest.* This is the interest from whatever shows in his bank account each month. The easiest (but not extremely accurate) way to figure this is to divide your interest rate by twelve, and multiply that by the account balance. So an account bearing 3 percent interest on a $1,500 balance would pay $3.75, or $(.03 \div 12) \times \$1,500$.
- *Salary.* My hypothetical entrepreneur stayed at his job full-time the first month, switched to half-time the second, and then bailed on the job entirely.

The Key to Everything—Cash Flow

The Small Business Development Center I attended in graduate school had all its students repeating a mantra at our first class until we went glassy-eyed: "cash is king." Keep repeating those words as you figure the numbers at the bottom of your pro forma. They're easily the most important figures of the entire exercise.

Start the first month with the amount of money you have in the bank—in our hypothetical entrepreneur's case, this is $300. Add the income for the month, subtract the expenses, and you're left with your cash on hand at the end of the month. Move that figure to the top of the small column in the next month. Trace this out for the year, and you can see how much cash you'll have at any given time. It doesn't matter if you've got a hundred clients lined up with orders next month if this month's cash on hand is below zero.

The Cash on Hand section of the spreadsheet represents your cash flow. When your income—that is, money you have already received, not money you're owed—is way over your expenses and you've got a cushion of money in the bank, this is no problem. But when your checking balance starts dipping toward zero, you'll need to do some major scrambling. Watching your profitability and your cash flow equally is the eternal price of entrepreneurship.

My business has been consistently profitable since about five months after it started, but I've had no fewer than four occasions where I've had to pull off a miracle to keep from bouncing rent checks and losing my phone service. It didn't matter that on paper I had nearly $2,000 coming to me. Until that check was deposited and cleared in my account, I couldn't spend it. The only thing that saved me one time was the arrival of an unexpected Visa card in the mail the day before an expense check was due—which saved my ass through the wonders of cash advance.

Times that require miracles take a major toll in stress and loss of personal equilibrium. The only cure is a cash cushion—which is more important during the start-up phase than any other time. You might be able to survive without it, as I did, but I can't recommend counting on miracles.

Fixing the First Draft

Our first draft has some obvious problems with it. Primary among those is bankruptcy in November and even further into the hole the following month.

There are three other less obvious issues, however. The first is is month-to-month cash flow. Although the plan doesn't go into the red until the end of the year, in January and from June onward the expenses exceed the cash on hand at the start of each month. If all the bills come due on the tenth and the checks don't come in until the thirtieth, our guy faces financial oblivion six months ahead of schedule. Note that he can stick to the plan in terms of income and expenses, and *still* run into serious cash issues. From June onward, he's in a serious cash crunch, and it's only a matter of time before the crash.

Second, I've zeroed out the automobile expenses, but there's no other budget item for transportation. Unless my hypothetical entrepreneur sprouts wings, he's going to be doing a lot of walking.

Third, and the most dangerous, there's no money budgeted into savings for the taxes on existing income. We have money going out in April for last year's taxes, but no money saved for the taxes we'll need for this year's income.

Table 2, "Sample Pro Forma, Revised," shows the plan with these problems fixed. Our entrepreneur scraped together another $1,000 for his start-up funds, which keep him from declaring bankruptcy. A new line item for transportation has been added, budgeting a $2 round-trip twenty days a month.

Quarterly tax payments have been included; in April, July, and October he budgets 15 percent of his client income from the previous three months for taxes. April is higher than that because he still has to include for last year (breaking down as $150 for the previous year, plus 15 percent of $0 + $250 + $250, which comes out to $225). In January of next year, which is off the chart, his tax payment for October, November, and December of this year will be $375. Income from his parents counts as gifts and is not taxable income.

Meanwhile, he's cut down on other expenses as best as possible. Bad debt has been reduced to 3 percent, more on a wish and a prayer than any other reason. He delays paying benefits for six months, during which time he'll be uninsured, have to cross the streets very carefully, and give up

TABLE 2 Sample Pro Forma, Revised

	Jan	Feb	Mar	Apr	May	Jun	Jul	Aug	Sep	Oct	Nov	Dec
Personal Expenses												
Auto	0	0	0	0	0	0	0	0	0	0	0	0
Bank charges	5	5	5	5	5	5	5	5	5	5	5	5
Child care	0	0	0	0	0	0	0	0	0	0	0	0
Clothing	200	20	20	20	20	100	20	20	20	20	20	20
Education	65	65	65	65	65	65	65	65	65	65	65	65
Entertainment	10	10	15	15	20	20	30	30	40	40	50	50
Gifts	0	0	0	0	30	30	0	0	0	0	0	50
Groceries	40	40	40	40	40	40	40	40	40	40	40	40
Household	20	20	20	20	20	20	20	20	20	20	20	20
Miscellaneous	20	20	20	20	20	20	20	20	20	20	20	20
Recreation	0	0	0	0	0	0	0	0	0	0	0	0
Rent	425	425	425	425	425	425	435	435	435	435	435	435
Restaurants	20	20	25	25	30	30	40	40	50	50	60	60
Subscriptions	0	0	0	0	0	0	0	0	0	0	0	0
Taxes	0	0	0	225	0	0	240	0	0	315	0	0
Telephone	50	50	50	60	60	60	70	70	70	80	80	80
Transportation	40	40	40	40	40	40	40	40	40	40	40	40
Travel	0	0	0	0	100	0	0	0	0	0	0	0
Utilities	0	0	0	0	0	0	0	0	0	0	0	100
Total Personal	$895	$715	$725	$960	$875	$855	$1,025	$785	$805	$1,130	$835	$985
Business Expenses												
Advertising	75	75	75	75	75	75	125	125	125	125	125	125
Bad debt	0	7.50	7.50	15	15	18	18	22.5	22.5	27	27	32
Benefits	0	0	0	0	0	0	75	75	75	75	75	75
Cost of goods	0	0	0	0	0	0	0	0	0	0	0	0
Dues	0	0	0	0	0	0	0	0	0	0	0	0

	Jan	Feb	Mar	Apr	May	Jun	Jul	Aug	Sep	Oct	Nov	Dec
Entertainment	20	20	20	20	30	30	30	30	40	40	40	40
Insurance	0	0	0	0	0	0	0	0	0	0	0	0
Interest	0	0	0	0	0	0	0	0	0	0	0	0
Janitorial	0	0	0	0	0	0	0	0	0	0	0	0
L & P fees	200	0	0	0	0	0	0	0	0	0	0	100
Rent	0	0	0	0	0	0	0	0	0	0	0	0
Returns	0	0	0	0	0	0	0	0	0	0	0	0
Supplies	50	20	20	20	20	20	20	20	20	20	20	20
Taxes	0	0	0	0	0	0	0	0	0	0	0	0
Telephone	0	0	0	0	0	0	0	0	0	165	15	15
Travel	0	0	0	0	0	0	0	0	0	0	0	0
Utilities	0	0	0	0	0	0	0	0	0	0	0	0
Wages	0	0	0	0	0	100	100	100	100	100	100	100
Total Business	$345	$123	$123	$130	$140	$143	$368	$373	$383	$552	$402	$507
Total Expenses	$1,240	$838	$848	$1,090	$1,015	$998	$1,393	$1,158	$1,188	$1,682	$1,237	$1,014
Income												
Bonuses	0	0	0	0	0	0	0	0	0	0	0	0
Client fees	0	250	250	500	500	600	600	750	750	900	900	1050
Family support	500	500	500	500	500	500	250	250	250	250	250	250
Gross sales	0	0	0	0	0	0	0	0	0	0	0	0
Interest	3.25	5.16	6.83	6.60	6.39	6.37	6.64	5.30	4.92	4.46	3.14	2.94
Salary	1500	750	0	0	0	0	0	0	0	0	0	0
Total Income	$2,003	$1,505	$757	$1,007	$1,006	$1,106	$857	$1,005	$1,005	$1,154	$1,153	$1,303
Cash on Hand												
Balance	1,300	2,063	2,730	2,639	2,556	2,547	2,655	2,119	1,966	1,783	1,255	1,171
Income	2,003	1,505	757	1,007	1,006	1,106	857	1,005	1,005	1,154	1,153	1,303
Expenses	1,240	838	848	1,090	1,015	998	1,393	1,158	1,188	1,682	1,237	1,014
End of Month	$2,063	$2,730	$2,639	$2,556	$2,547	$2,655	$2,119	$1,966	$1,783	$1,255	$1,171	$1,460

contact sports. Entertainment has been reduced to a slower growth curve. Legal and professional fees have been zeroed in April, since the taxes for the previous year will be fairly simple. He delays installing the new phone line for three months, and cancels his business trip in June.

On the income side, he projects client fees to grow more rapidly. Again, this is a wish-and-a-prayer number; although $1,050 isn't all that much to make in a month's time, it's a substantial boost from zero at the beginning of the year. The business growth curve in our first plan is more realistic than the one in the second, but the second one isn't out of the realm of possibility.

Our second plan still has some financial difficulties toward the end of the year. The solution is another revision with lower expenses or a higher projected income. The latter is the easy way out—and a dangerous path to take if your projections are too rosy. Cutting costs is always the surer bet.

Into the Future

Formal business plans require this financial projection to be continued for at least three years. For less formal plans, you can do this as a mental exercise if you like, but in my estimation that would be a waste of time. It'd be far more helpful to come back and do it after you've run the business for six months and you have that experience under your belt.

For years two and three, generally all that is required is a breakdown by quarter, not by month. You can build a quarterly plan for your first year by going through every line, adding the figures in January through March, and then putting that sum in a new column called Q1. Do the same for April through June, July through September, and October through December, creating new columns called Q2, Q3, and Q4. These new columns are your quarterly plan for this year.

Then extend that out by following numeric trends, and make a forecast for the next two years. Remember to flatten out your growth curves as you go. If you think your business will double in your second six months, project an increase of only 50 percent over the course of year two and 25 percent over year three. Nudge up your expenses as necessary to match, keeping direct and indirect cost increases in mind the entire way.

In the end, your numbers will probably be way off from where you'll be in three years, but if it makes you start thinking about the long term, that can help you hit your goals.

Building the Grubstake

Now that you know how much money you'll need to kick off your business safely, there remains the issue of actually socking it away. Short of selling your soul, you've got six basic options for raising cash.

First is the most unglamorous: get a job, or hold onto the one you've already got. Yes, even if you've already decided to quit first thing tomorrow morning, the fact remains that a steady paycheck is the surest path to setting money aside. Salaries also have the nice feature that you won't have to pay them back, which is more than can be said of loans.

Make your period of indenture easier by knowing exactly how much you'll need to save and setting a definite number of months you'll work to get there. Put away the proper amount each month, and don't touch it come hell or high water. In the meantime, research everything there is to know about your business.

Second, you can root around to see if you have anything you can pawn. Many twentysomethings with middle-class or wealthier backgrounds have stock or bonds that were purchased back in the days of disco. Ask your parents if there's anything left in old safe-deposit boxes with your name on it, and let them know you've got a good reason for cashing in those assets.

Also, a fair number of us have squirreled away memorabilia from our childhoods that is worth big bucks to collectors. A collector is a polite term for someone who looks normal but is willing to spend thousands of dollars for your garbage. When I was four or five I had a complete set of Star Trek dolls and an Enterprise with a working transporter. (Well, the transporter was more like a plastic box, but I had an active imagination.) A few years ago I was at a Star Trek convention—yes, I'll admit it—and saw those same damn toys for $100 a pop. Check your closets for comic books, product giveaways, movie posters, toys, dolls, and anything else that you've been meaning to unload for years. Then head down to a well-stocked magazine rack and look through the publications dedicated to those items. You should quickly get a sense for whether what you have is fabulous riches or as valuable as old Spam. If you've got anything good, the magazines will list dealers who will buy from you. Expect to get 10 to 25 percent of what the magazine quotes as its value.

And if anyone is sitting on pre-1978 Amazing Spider-Mans they want to sell cheap, give me a call.

Third, you can go to the First National Bank of Mom and Dad, or any relatives or close friends who you think might back you. Money from these sources is generally interest-free or at least low-interest—in the financial sense anyway. Unfortunately, these loans are frequently high-interest in the sense that your lenders will take a high interest in your business. By taking their money, you are giving them a license to meddle in your business and in your life until every dime is paid back. You might have some relatives for whom this is not a problem, but all of us have family members who could make our lives a living hell. Decide before you take their cash whether you want to risk this.

Fourth, if people aren't willing to give you loans, they might be willing to buy shares. That's what the partnership idea is all about. If you have a few partnership nibbles, call an attorney and ask for some pointers on getting one started.

Fifth, call the Small Business Association. They shell out around $40 million a day for new businesses—and if they won't give you money, they'll help you find someone who will. Have a formal business plan ready or nearly so—they'll expect to see something professional.

Sixth, you can try doing what everyone else does: go to a bank. Frankly, someone with our age and lack of experience has a better chance of hitting the Lotto than getting a loan from most banks. But it can't hurt to try. Write a formal business plan, apply for the loan, and when they turn you down, pump them for as much information as possible about how you can improve your business plan for the next bank. If you properly apply what you learn, you may eventually find some cash.

The End Product

If you've made it through all that, congratulations. If you've just skimmed this chapter and haven't yet picked up a pencil, don't let it unduly stress you. Sure, writing a business plan is a lot of work, but remember that it doesn't have to be any more formal than you need it to be. Your first business plan can be handwritten on a few sheets of paper after a day's research at the library.

How much effort you'll put into planning is up to you. The readers who have done the work in this chapter will have a much more intimate understanding of their businesses than those who skipped it. The more work you do in advance, the better off you'll be when you hit the ground running.

CHAPTER 7

Thinking and Acting Like a Pro

*N*ow that you've got a plan, or the semblance of one, it's time to start talking the talk and walking the walk. Running a successful business is a mixture of style and substance. Since we all know that looks count for more than brains, we'll start with the right appearances to get things going.

It's Not What You Know, It's Where You Are

The right location is immensely important to any business. When I started my business, I thought I was location-proof. After all, my plan was to sell computer services from a home office. I figured any place in any city would do me equally well. So when I moved to Washington, the main thing on my mind when I rented my apartment was that it was a block from the woman I was dating. (She broke up with me before I moved in. Par for the course.)

Three years later, though, a large chunk of my business—frequently the majority of my business—comes from a local network of home-based businesses that meets two blocks from my apartment. If I had moved a mile farther south, I never would have heard of the meetings, I never would have found that block of prospects and clients—and I never would have written this book, since I met my literary agent at the first meeting. It's clear in my mind that if I hadn't lucked into my location, my business would have been a very different story.

Think about the sort of work you will be doing, and how you envision yourself meeting clients and making sales. Does your business need to take place in an office? In a store? In your customers' houses? Somewhere else entirely?

Once you have a handle on the answers, you can decide which kind of business space you want. The first option is the "traditional" business, run out of a store or office. For some product-based businesses, there's no alternative to incurring the costs of a store. And there's no question these spaces are the most respected and commonly accepted places to do business. But since you'll be paying rent twice—once for your home and once for your business—it's a pricey way to get started. The second option is setting up a home office. This has seen a massive boom in recent years, mainly driven by people who have found their bosses to be far more tolerable when they are miles away. Thanks to new equipment geared for the SOHO (Small Office-Home Office) market, there's very little you can do in a traditional office that you can't do with home-office technology.

The third option is renting office space from a business incubator. Business incubators are either run as private businesses or sponsored by a local Small Business Development Center. In return for a nominal fee, usually about $50 a month, you get to use the incubator's phone number, fax machine, secretarial services, and office and meeting space when you need it. Your business phone number is unique; when a client calls, she probably won't be able to tell that she's not calling a traditional office. Since all the resources are shared, some incubators are better than others for providing consistent, quality services to their clients—but that beats worrying about your housemates or little sister answering the phone when a business call comes through.

There's No Place Like Home

I'm willing to go out on a limb and say that a home office is the easiest route for the majority of under-financed twenty-somethings starting businesses. There are some businesses that definitely won't fly at home—a mechanized car wash, for example. But with some ingenuity and flexibility in your business design, the home office can be made to fit just about anyone's business needs.

Home offices require more self-control than traditional businesses. After all, while you're slaving away in a small corner, your television, books, and Sega video game are beckoning from the next room. It's also much easier to let your working hours slip by sleeping in late or knocking off early.

Working at home has a way of magnifying the entrepreneur's flaws—and all of us have them. Working by yourself in a familiar environment, there's less impetus to break your bad habits. If you don't have the discipline to force yourself to work under these conditions, a home office is a decidedly bad idea.

Self-discipline is only one part of your psyche that may reflect whether you'll do well working from home. Entrepreneurs who live and work by themselves may be prone to loneliness and depression. If your home office is in a shared living space, you may hate the lack of privacy and the disturbances caused by your housemates. And any entrepreneur will find that a home office encourages the creeping expansion of his work day to every waking hour. A few weeks ago my business phone rang at 1 A.M., and my first thought was, "Who's calling me at this hour?" But without quite meaning to, I had already instinctively picked up the phone and said, "Hello, Millennium." Events like that have a way of eating into your life.

But you can't beat the price. Later, when your business is profitable enough to justify it, you can move to an outside space if you've found working at home to be constricting. Personally, I've gotten so used to it that I'd go nuts if I ever had more than a thirty-second commute.

Picking the Right Spot

Even if you're working from home, there's good reason to consider moving to find the proper place to start a business.

The first reason is that where you're living now might not have a space that's suited for business needs. If you're terminally organized, perhaps you can handle having your personal and business life mixed up in a one-room apartment, but I've never been that skillful. My first apartment in Washington was small, but I picked it because it had a large walk-in closet and a foyer. First the closet and then the foyer became my "office" as I tested out layouts that worked. I had to climb over my office chair to get into the apartment sometimes, but I had something resembling an office.

The second reason you might want to move is what we mentioned before: you must find a location that's conducive to the business you'll do. A carver of stone gargoyles had better not live in a five-story walk-up. A home-based desktop publisher will have problems with walk-in traffic if there's a Kinko's Copies across the street.

Think of the ways you expect to generate business. If you're picturing a busy store filled with walk-in traffic, you can rule out a home-based business. On the other hand, if you plan to manufacture products that you can ship by mail

S o, you ask, how do you find an area with mail-order shoppers, or any other bit of arcane information that I'm telling you to research?

These questions usually require combining information from a few sources. For example, for the mail-order idea, first I would check census data and public records on the real-estate values in a particular target area. Then I would find marketing research that correlates income to shopping habits, which you could find in a business library at a nearby university or Small Business Development Center. My results would have a high margin of error—families in $120,000 homes in Manhattan probably have different shopping habits than people in similarly priced homes in Utah—but it would at least give me some ideas. If research has never been your strong point, get over to a Small Business Administration office or Small Business Development Center and ask for some assistance.

order, you're in business. Just find someplace to store your products and start circulating catalogs—all you need at home is a telephone. And it would save you plenty of time and money if you could locate your home office in an area where people do a lot of shopping by mail order, since you could hand-deliver catalogs a block at a time and determine which areas are worth pursuing as rich in customers.

The perfect location for any business is Right There—the spot where a prospective customer will find you just as they are thinking about the products or services you sell. It's nice to fantasize about having products so renowned that customers will drive hundreds of miles to buy from you, but it takes far too much money in marketing, and of course an exceptional product, to have that kind of clientele. Don't make it difficult for your customers to buy from you. Put your business where they are, and don't ask them to go out of their way.

Make certain that you know the idiosyncrasies of the area you're in. I interviewed a former entrepreneur who set up shop at a convenient location only a few blocks from a large residential area that had no one else providing his service—a medical product that a substantial number of people in the area needed. He figured that since he was nearby, people would walk to his location because it was more convenient than driving to a competitor.

It was an uphill battle all the way. He was from a northern urban area and thought nothing of walking several blocks to go shopping; his customers routinely drove to malls, which is where his competition was. He could have opened his office next door to one of theirs and faced less competition from them than he did at his location. As it was, the others offered a convenience that he had overlooked.

Getting Permission from the Locals

If you're shopping for a new apartment to launch a home-based business, check into the local zoning laws that might affect you. Some communities absolutely, under no circumstances, allow home-based businesses, but such places are growing rarer. With a service-based business, you should have no problem, but if you will be meeting clients, storing products, or making sales at your home, you could run into legal problems. A local library or SBA office can tell you if your desired location is kosher for your needs.

The Clothes Make the Money

Imagine yourself at a business networking meeting looking for a computer consultant who can work with your staff and bring about some rapid change. After mingling for a little while, you meet two consultants. The first is me; I'm dressed in a navy double-breasted suit and a red tie with an intriguing design—tame enough not to be called loud, at least not to my face. The other is wearing wrinkled pants and a blue turtleneck with tears in the shoulder stitching that are visible from several feet away. His hair is plastered down to his head, and his heavy-framed glasses make eye contact impossible. All you can see is that huge stripe across his eyebrows.

So, who are you going to hire? If your budget is small and you're looking for someone who's willing to work for food, you'll go with my competition. That's fine with me; if your budget is that low, I don't want you as a client. But I will make a point of talking to you for a few minutes so you'll know I'm around when you can afford me—and thanks to my appearance, you won't be surprised when the price I quote is five times what the other guy charges.

Ask anyone who's known me for more than fifteen minutes, and they'll tell you I'm not a fashion plate. My girlfriend is constantly on my back for forgetting to comb my hair, and I'll put off doing laundry until I'm down to the bottom of my T-shirt drawer. But I've always had a knack for dress clothes, and that instinct has paid off for me.

The trick is to dress a little better than the guy next to you. The definition of the word "better" will depend entirely on your clientele—if you sell skateboards, for all I know that might mean your Metallica shirt has been fashionably scuffed by your nipple ring. And key on the words "a little" better. Overdressing is just as much a sin as underdressing—and the surest way of turning off potential clients. There are thousands of rules for dressing right, and hundreds of thousands of ways to selectively break them and really make a stunning impression. The best way to learn them is to actively study the clothing selections of people in your professional circles who dress well. Get the opinions of your friends and business associates. Read business magazines—or the magazines that your clients read—to get an idea of what the well-dressed entrepreneur in your field is wearing.

Skip *GQ, Vogue,* and the other fashion magazines. You can feed a family of four for what one of those undershirts cost. There's also a serious risk in wearing bleeding-edge fashion amongst the unwashed masses who are not as style-conscious.

Once you have an idea of what to wear, try buying it at secondhand stores, Salvation Army and thrift shops, and consignment stores. All of these will give you the opportunity to walk out with some truly hideous clothing, but regular browsing of their wares—pun not intended—should turn up a gem every once in a while.

Accessorizing Is Not Just Gold and Diamonds

Your clothes are only half your appearance. The other half is what you carry.

I was once approached at a business mingle by a guy who offered to analyze my phone records and show me the best way to save money on my calls. Now, my phone records give away a lot of information about what I do and where I am. Some serious trust must be established before I'll even think about giving anybody that business. He was also selling other telephone-based products, and talked the talk about high-powered communications. I said I would have to think about it; could I have his cellular phone number so I could contact him in a hurry?

When he didn't have a cellular phone, he didn't get my sale. It had nothing to do with reaching him immediately—but anyone who is selling those services had better be a user of them, or have an excellent explanation for why not.

I am an Internet consultant. My panoply of gadgets includes a laptop computer with an internal modem, portable hard drive, and portable printer. I can set up a more or less complete office out of my carry-on bag just about anywhere I go. I rarely do—but all of my clients know that I can. I have a phone number that follows me anywhere in the world. On a recent road trip, I gave it out to a dozen clients. None of them called me and interrupted my trip so there was no loss for me, but all of them knew that they could reach me if necessary.

OK, so I'm starting to sound like a propeller head with a jet helicopter hovering in the parking lot. The point is that in your business you have to carry the things that demonstrate your qualifications and single-minded interest in what you do. I want to meet writers with pen and paper; freelance journalists with tape recorders; desktop publishers with exceptional brochures; musicians with top-of-the-line CD Walkmans. Entrepreneurs who sell personal products should be walking billboards, within the bounds of good taste. It all adds up to lending an air of assurance to your work and your product, and building confidence with the customer.

Getting Wired

Writing the business plan should have been enough to convince you: running a business is heavy on number-crunching and document preparation. People like me, who find it more natural to write on a keyboard than with anything as archaic as a pen, regularly thank their lucky stars for having a mechanical beast to do the heavy lifting when it comes to mundane chores. I get antsy if it's been more than twelve hours since I've checked my electronic mail.

For the rest of you who are not computer geeks, though, it's probably not as clear why you should you be using a computer, let alone why you should be using the Internet and online services. I'm going to take a few pages to try to convince you.

Reason One: Paper Sucks

Every chapter of this book brings up new reasons why you need to keep documentation about your business. It's stunning how much needs to be recorded—everything from notes on budget planning to documenting down to the penny the exact amount you've spent, not to mention records of every phone call and letter, and meeting with clients and prospects along the way.

When you start a business, your life becomes a document trail. Some people are very efficient at generating these documents in paper-and-ink form, and keeping track of it all—but that sort of meticulousness is a dying art.

If you expect to make a go of this with a few Bic pens, a ream of paper, and your old Selectric typewriter, I can't tell you that it won't work. But it's an inefficient way of going about your life. On a typewriter, columns of figures don't automatically generate totals, documents cannot be easily changed, and you're stuck with using manila folders and a Xerox machine to keep track of it all.

Computers are a much better tool for this sort of thing. They cost a lot of money, and even more time, while you figure out how to use them to your best advantage. But, in my opinion, it's money and time very well invested.

Reason Two: Professionalism Costs Money— A Little or a Lot

When I was in high school, the state of the art method of getting information on paper was a dot-matrix printer. It was slow and loud, and what showed up on paper was pretty much garbage by today's standards. Of course, it was possible to buy printers that promised "near-letter quality," which was a blunt admission that what we ended up with was not as good as what came out of a typewriter. For a few thousand bucks, you could get a daisy-wheel printer, which was basically an automated typewriter. It looked as good as a typewritten document, but it was so expensive that only a few businesses could afford it. As a result, enough paper was floating about with dot-matrix print that it was accepted as proper business documentation.

Today, laser printers start at around $500; you can get something close to laser quality for $200. People are starting to notice the difference between text printed at 300 dots per inch and text printed at 600 dots per inch; the former, which seemed to be miraculously high quality five years ago, is now the standard norm of business documentation.

This has raised the standard of what is considered acceptable for a business document. With such high quality available at such a low cost, your clients today will expect proportional text, where each character takes up a different amount of space. They'll expect multiple font sizes and typefaces. They'll expect documents with no errors, proper margins, and easy readability. That means your correspondence, invoices, business cards, brochures, and anything else you generate must meet these expectations. Handwritten memos won't cut it, and neither will a typewritten document with obvious spots of Liquid Paper.

You'll have to meet these standards, and there are two ways to do it. First, you could give all your documents to a print shop, which will gladly charge you $30 for a pack of letters, or a few hundred for a brochure or other marketing document. Or you can get a computer and do it yourself.

It doesn't matter whether what you're selling is decidedly low-tech. You'll still have to communicate what your business can do to your customers and prospects. Many of these people will tune you right out if what arrives in their hands is shoddy and second-rate. The best way to prevent that is to do it yourself, and get it done right.

Reason Three: You Can't Get to Heaven on a Typewriter Ribbon

I've been expounding on the usefulness of the Internet for a while now in marginal commentary. If you've been skipping those parts as your eyes glazed over, here's the essential summary.

There are around thirty million people using the Internet worldwide. Depending upon who you ask, that number will break 100 million either by the end of this decade or sometime next Tuesday. Among those millions are people who have a lot to teach you based on their own experiences or their own cultures. You can't beat that sort of opportunity with a stick—and it can be invaluable for your business.

The Internet gives you the power to communicate with people worldwide instantly and at no per-call cost. Got friends in Europe? Stop calling them and talk to them by e-mail; save your phone money for food and business materials. Wondering if your product will sell in California? Don't fly there—teleport there using the Internet and talk to as many natives as you can. Need to research just about any question raised over the course of doing business? There's some resource on the Net that can help.

The Internet is where this book would be if it were written over a period of twenty years by a few million authors who violently disagree. On it, you'll find all the information, argument, and nuance that can't fit into a book of any length.

The First Step: Getting the Computer

All of that is very well and good, you're probably thinking, but computers cost a lot of money, and I expect most of yours right now is earmarked for luxuries such as food and shelter. So first decide what you want, and then find the cheapest way of laying your hands on it.

The dirty little secret of the computer industry is that you don't need what they're selling. Computers are caught in an economic spiral where the companies that make them deliberately replace everything on the market with something that's vastly more powerful every twelve months, sometimes faster. The machines that are being sold today are literally three or four times better than what was on the shelves a year ago. If automobiles were made the same way, you could drive from Los Angeles to Boston on a few gallons of gas.

What this means is that computers that were state of the art circa 1989 are pretty much perfectly good right now—if you're willing to give up the frills that the computer industry tries to make you believe are essential. On the flip side, however, there *is* such a thing as too old. You want to make sure that what you have can do what you need it to.

At this point, it would be very easy to drown you in computerese and useless technical terms and numbers. Instead, I'm going to boil it down to a single component: the operating system. The operating system (sometimes called OS) determines what programs the computer can use, and to a large extent what those programs look like on the computer screen. All operating systems have minimum requirements in order to be used on a particular computer. We're going to exploit that fact to make sure that you get a computer that's good enough, even if you don't know anything else about what goes into the machine.

There are two basic flavors of computers: Macs (and Macintosh clones, made by companies other than Apple Computer) and PCs (Personal Computers—which are either IBM or IBM PC clones). If you want a PC, you'll be looking for an operating system called Microsoft Windows 3.1.

You've probably heard the hype about the replacement for Windows 3.1, which is called Windows 95. Windows 95 is definitely easier to use and more powerful, but it also requires a much more powerful computer, for which you'd have to pay extra. On the Macintosh side, the operating system is called System 7. There are newer versions of this—they're up to 7.5.3 as I write this—but again, the higher numbers require the bigger bucks. A computer running Windows 3.1 or System 7 will do you just fine.

The problem with recommending last year's computers is that most stores sell this year's computers, at this year's prices. To pick up an older computer, you need to either buy it used, or get a model that's on factory closeout. Factory closeouts occur when a company needs to clear out its warehouses of last year's models to make way for the newer, bigger, and more expensive systems. They need to move a lot of equipment, and they don't much care what they sell it for.

I definitely recommend the factory closeout route. You'll get a new computer, if not a new model. The warranty will be intact, the boxes and cables will all be there, and it will be much easier to get technical support when you're the first owner. Factory closeout models change rapidly, but you can frequently pick up a complete system for between $500 and $1,000. The best places to start are computer catalogs. You'll find dozens listed in the back of any computer magazine, but here are a few to get you started:

Macintosh catalogs
MacMall: (800) 222-2808; MacZone: (800) 248-0800
MacSystems Warehouse: (800) 558-4364

IBM catalogs
Damark: (800) 729-9000; PC Zone: (800) 258-2088
PC Connection: (800) 800-1111

Used computers are an even cheaper way to go. In some cases you can find usable used computer machines for less than $200. The problem with used computers is similar to that of used cars: Lord only knows what you'll get. Most computers have a life span long enough that they can pass to second owners and still work fine, but there are lemons in every lot. Beware especially of computers being sold by previous owners with pets, small children, or who smoke, since computers do not get along well with any of the above. If you buy used, try to do so from someone you trust, or at least bring along a friend who's knowledgeable in these things and can check out the system for you. If you can't do that, consider saving your pennies until you can afford something fresh out of the box.

A third option for the very lucky is the freebie. Call family and friends, especially the business types, and find out if they have a computer they're not using or that they're about to replace. It's a long shot, but it can save you a bundle if it works. Another freebie route is to use nearby campus computer labs or a friend's system, but I recommend against it. You'll have too much riding on it to leave up to chance whether you'll be able to use it when you need it.

Incidentally, if you're totally confused about what kind of computer to get, I recommend the Macintosh. Macs are easier to use—and to care for and feed—than IBM systems, especially if the computer you're getting is eligible for Social Security. For basic business purposes, either will do the job, but Macs can be a lot less frustrating for computer neophytes.

Step Two: The Software You'll Need

Computers without software are like a fifteen-year-old watching MTV. All the machinery is there, but no neurons are firing. You'll need to toss something more into the system to get it to work for you.

There are approximately 100,000 software programs available. You need two: a decent word-processing program and a good financial planner. A word processor is a typewriter on steroids: the document can be edited as many times as you like so that it comes out picture perfect. You can also save a basic business document, such as an invoice, and print it out with modifications for various customers and clients. The financial planner, on the other hand, is what you'll use to keep track of your business expenses, income, and all the other information that keeps the IRS from hounding you.

If you purchased one of the complete home-system kind of computers, it probably came with just about everything you need pre-installed. Otherwise, you'll have to order the software separately. The best place to do this is from one of the catalog vendors listed above. Their prices are frequently cheaper than in computer stores.

For a word processor, your best bet is either Microsoft Works or ClarisWorks. Both are low-priced (around $100 to $150) and come with a kitchen sink of software—a word processor, drawing program, spreadsheet (for mathematical and financial calculations, such as your pro formas), database (for keeping track of clients and other information), and a few others depending upon which version you get.

The financial-planning software market is dominated by a program called Quicken. It's a very good program; what few flaws can be found in it are usually fixed in the next version the following year. The first time you buy a copy, expect to pay $40 to $60; the upgrades every year are around $20 and are well worth it.

Whatever you do, do not—I repeat, *do not*—have a friend come by and dump a whole bunch of software onto your computer so you don't have to buy any. I'm not telling you this because it's immoral, and I'm not telling you this because it's illegal. I'm telling you this because it's stupid. I've had many clients who have had to pay me big bucks to fix the damage done by friends doing them favors. Illegally copied software comes with no manuals and probably is missing some files that you won't know you need until it's too late.

If all of your software is legally purchased, and someone mentions that they put some "fun stuff" on your computer, tell them to strip it right back off. Until you feel comfortable with your system, don't let anybody monkey with it—or you'll end up calling someone like me and I'll put you on the clock.

Step Three: Getting Online

Nowadays, 90 percent of the reason to own a computer is to be on the Internet or an online service. By itself, the computer is a glorified calculator and typewriter; with the addition of a small plastic box and a telephone line, it's your link to the rest of the world.

You need a piece of equipment called a modem to get online. The modem acts as the translator between the signals that your computer understands and the signals that can be sent over a standard telephone wire. The modem is either a small box that sits next to the computer, or is on a special "card" that is internally installed in your computer. If you purchased one of those all-in-one systems that came with the monitor, keyboard, and software, there's an excellent chance that a modem came with it as well.

There are several types of modems, distinguished mainly by their communication speeds and their ability to work with fax machines. Modems are measured in "baud rates." A baud is a measure of digital information; a character of text uses about ten baud to get where it's going. So the previous sentence, which is 108 characters long, would take about a half-second to transmit on a 2400 baud-modem—the slowest-speed modem that can be purchased these days.

In modems as in cars, faster is better. There is no way of knowing how much information you'll be trafficking once you're up and running on the Net. Some people stick to tasks that require only low baud rates, such as electronic mail. Others go for the fancy graphics, video, and audio on the World Wide Web, for which many people feel even the fastest modems available today are too slow.

If you have a little money to spend, your choice narrows down to two speeds: 14,400 baud and 28,800 baud. The latter, usually just called 28.8, is the fastest modem commonly available, and usually runs in the $150 to $200 range. A 14.4 modem can often be found for less than $100. I recommend

---

Internet

Fax-modems provide three other handy features. First, since the image for the fax is generated inside the computer, it comes out perfectly on the other end—none of the jagged edges or poor reproductions that can be seen when you have to pump paper through a machine on the sending side. Second, incoming images go right into the computer, so you don't have to deal with that repulsive, curly thermal fax paper. And last, many fax software programs come with a feature called optical character recognition. This takes an incoming fax and converts it to text that you can edit yourself. It's not perfect, but it's a lot faster than retyping documents yourself.

to all my clients that, if it's not a hardship, they should go with the 28.8; there's no way of telling how much time you'll save later, and if you value your time at all, you'll make back the extra money very quickly.

The other option to look for is fax capability. (See sidebar.) Most new modems either have it or don't, but some older models may only be able to send faxes, not receive. With a little shopping, you should be able to find a brand of fax-modem that costs no more than modems of the same speed without fax capability. Many more people have fax machines than are online—so far—so it's an incredible time-saver to have the fax-modem right on board the computer. It's also a lot cheaper than buying a full-fledged fax machine.

Once you have the modem, just plug it into the computer (a fifteen-second procedure on a Mac, sometimes much longer on an IBM), then plug in the phone wire. If your modem has two phone jacks on the back, you can plug a regular phone into the other jack and let the phone and the modem share the line. You can use your regular phone line for modem and fax use, although whenever the computer is using the phone, you won't be able to.

Your last step is to get yourself onto an online service. There are two ways of getting wired. First, you could subscribe to a commercial online service like CompuServe, America Online, or Prodigy. Second, you could find an Internet service provider (abbreviated ISP) and get direct access to the Internet. The advantage of the online services is that they control everything that happens on their systems, which makes learning the ropes a lot easier. You'll pay a premium for this, though. Some online services charge as much as $3 an hour.

Going with an ISP is frequently cheaper. Many will give you unlimited access for less than $30 a month, or will give you something like sixty hours a month for $20. The downside is that you'll be using the Internet directly, which can be daunting for first-timers. For many, the best way to proceed is to start with a commercial service to learn the ropes, then consider adding or switching to an ISP.

To use either a commercial online service or an ISP, you'll need to get its software. America Online and Compu-Serve give out so many free disks to hook subscribers that some of my clients don't buy disks anymore; they just wipe the ones that AOL sends them. Call their 800 numbers to get the software, or open any computer magazine and pick up one of the dozen small cards that fall on the floor.

What's This Internet, Anyway?

The Internet is a DNA-spliced, mutant clone of the Encyclopedia Galactica, Romper Room, and Arkham Asylum (of "Batman" fame). Essentially, it is a set of standards by which any computer in the world can tap into a pipeline and talk to any other computer connected to the pipeline.

This makes all thirty-odd million Internet users self-publishers. The content that's available on the Net is the sum total of what all these people think is worth sharing. When that person is, say, an editor at *Time*, then what you'll read can be a worthwhile use of your time. When that person is an addled fifteen-year-old looking for nude pictures of Cindys Crawford and Brady, it can be pretty vile.

The trick with the Net is to find those people who have something useful to share, and ignore those who don't. Sounds like real life, doesn't it?

It can be pretty tedious ignoring all the people who blather on and on about worthless topics on the Net. But if you're worried about accidentally coming across something that you might find offensive, relax. It takes some know–how to get a XXX-rated picture to pop up on your screen—the chances of coming across something that is outside your bounds of decency is pretty slight. You'll come across salty language from time to time, but that's rather easily ignored. Once you're up and running, there's no end to the places you can go on the Net. If you want to read a book on the topic, take your pick: a recent informal count listed 1,300 books about the Internet, usually selling for $20 to $30 a pop. My recommendation: skip them all. (Except mine, when I write it.) Go directly online, and use the Internet's own resources to guide you.

A quick overview of common Internet uses will help you get started. Keep in mind that none of these things actually *is* the Internet. It's more accurate to say that the Internet is the infrastructure that allows all of these things to work.

- *Electronic Mail.* Possibly the coolest thing since the invention of gelato. An e-mail message is pretty simple: it consists of the text of the message, the place or places where it's headed, and a brief title or subject line that warns the reader what the letter is about. What makes this revolutionary is that once you send it, it'll get where it's going in anywhere from less than a second to a few hours. E-mail is so fast that I'll frequently read a message, send back a reply, and then get a reply *from the same person* before I'm done reading my next e-mail.

  Unlike regular mail—which the cognoscenti call "snail mail" thanks to its speedy delivery—it doesn't matter how far your mail goes, or how many people you send it to. With every Internet provider and most online services, mail is a total freebie. Write a letter and send it to a few thousand people if you like—with no stamps to buy and no glue taste on your tongue.

  E-mail is sent, no surprise here, to e-mail addresses. These look something like this: creative@getnet.com.

(The period at the end of the last sentence is not part of the e-mail address, but the period between "getnet" and "com" is.) "Creative" is the name of the recipient; "getnet.com" is the location where the recipient can be found. In this case, it's an Internet provider in Phoenix, Arizona, but that doesn't matter to you. You don't need to have any idea where a message is physically going to get it to the person you want to read it.

(Distance is like that on the Net; I spend plenty of time on my Arizona account, even though I'm several thousand miles away most of the time.)

- *The World Wide Web.* This is the bit that got everybody screaming in the last few years, and woke up the general public to what we geeks have known for years: the Net is massively cool. The Web links a few hundred million documents to one another in a format that's called hypertext. Hypertext lets you read something of interest and then click on a word or two and jump to more information about that topic. For example, in this paragraph the words "World Wide Web" might take you to a general index of the Web; the word "cool" might link to the "Cool Web Sites of the Day" list; and the word "geeks" might show you pictures of a few guys I knew in college.

  People are working all the time to expand the capabilities of the Web, which is partly why you see new multibillion-dollar companies springing up to take advantage of it. I can't even begin to tell you what's there. Best thing to do is fire up your Web software. It'll take you directly to a "home page" (tech-ese for starting point), and you can start browsing from there.

- *USENET.* If your idea of Heaven is appearing on one televised talk show after another until a Dustbuster is used to suck away your desiccated body, look no further. The USENET is a collection of about 15,000 discussion groups dedicated to just about every topic of discussion known to humankind. No fooling—everything from obscure computer programming to dead languages to bestiality and endless dissections of the news. Somewhere in there you'll find worthwhile stuff, as well, since the people using these groups include the bona fide experts who can help you with whatever you need to know. There have been numerous times when a client threw a question at me that I couldn't field; I simply posted a message to the appropriate USENET group and became an instant expert within twenty-four hours when kind souls replied to my questions.

There are about a dozen more major ways you can browse, search, and waste time on the Net. Start with these three, which can be the richest treasure troves, and then expand into a few others when you're more comfortable.

Papers? We Don't Need No Stinking Papers!

Well, actually, you do, and now that you've got the computer it'll be easier to put them together. Every business needs to communicate on paper, and every business should do so in a professional and clear style. This translates into stationery, cards, and brochures that will combine to give your business a professional image.

You first need to come up with either a logo or logotype. Common usage among my colleagues defines a logo as a small graphic picture that represents your business; a logotype does the same thing, but is made up of your company name in a distinctive combination of fonts and sizes. Logos and logotypes are not necessary to a business, but they can go a long way in creating a distinctive look that will remind customers about your business.

You can see my logotype in the upper left corner of figure 1, "Sample Invoice" on page 160. It's simply my company name in a font named Bank Gothic, which I italicized and then rearranged to get the spacing exactly the way I wanted it. The "C" in Consulting is lined up on a diagonal with the first "I" in Millennium, the idea being to convey a sense of forward motion. It was much easier to design than a logo; I still have no idea what a millennium would look like in a small drawing.

If you don't want to design a logo or logotype—or pay a designer a lot of money to do it for you—you don't have to. But you should pick a single font and type style (italic or bold, for example) that you will use to write the name of your company on all correspondence and public documents. Consistency is key in creating a professional image.

Your Future Is in These Cards

Back in Victorian times, it was an absolute must when visiting someone to hand their doorman a calling card announcing who you were. Today, in celebration of that ridiculous custom, we do the same thing.

A business card has a truly frightening effect on people. The difference between having and not having one is the difference between showing up at a wedding with or without your pants. Some people start new businesses simply by printing up a set of cards and taking them to a business social to see if anyone is interested. Not having one, or "running out," is basically announcing to your prospect that you're not serious about your business. Which is awfully embarrassing when you actually do run out.

If you have a decent printer, you can print business cards yourself, ten at a time using precut sheets. But why bother? Business cards are something you should hand out by the bushel; when a client asks you for cards to give to her professional contacts, you should give her a stack. The precut sheets are nice for doing a quick card that looks different, or for testing a new design, but in the long run they are not cost-effective.

If you want your logo or logotype on your business card, the going rate is about $30 for 500 cards. I did that at first, but decided later that the premium wasn't worth it. My local office-supply store offers 1,000 cards for $9, which makes it much easier to spread them around like popcorn. Instead of using my logo on my business cards, I had my business name printed in the same font that I use in my letterhead text. I would prefer to still have my logotype, but I haven't seen any negative effects from the switch.

Your business cards should contain all of the information clients need to remember you and get in touch with you. Phone number, fax, snail mail, and e-mail addresses are standard. Be sure to note which number is your phone line and which is your fax. If most of your clients and customers have never heard of the Internet, note on the card which address is for e-mail so the @ sign doesn't confuse them.

There are two conflicting ideas on what else to put on the card. Many marketers will say you should add information about your business; some even recommend special cards that fold out into mini-brochures. I'm of the mind that a card should be spartan. It puts the onus on me to make a memorable impression on a prospect. When I hand someone a card, I usually handwrite on the back some key points from our conversation and about my services, which serves as a more personalized reminder for them.

Once you have cards, use them. I always keep my wallet full so I can unload as many as I want when given the opportunity. Don't be one of those people who slip the card into the handshake before you even know the other guy's name, but do offer your card when you ask for someone else's. We'll talk more about business-card etiquette when we get to chutzpah in chapter 10.

Letter-Perfect Business Documents

Your next step is to design letterhead. An example of my letterhead can be found in figure 1. Upper left is my logotype; upper right is my address, phone number, and e-mail address. Your word-processing program will come with sample letterhead formats; you can work your way through the manual to learn how to design your own.

Some people dash right out and purchase preprinted letterhead along with their business cards. It's nice to have paper with raised lettering, but I've never thought the expense to be worth it. Get your business cards done professionally because they can do large quantities cheaply and easily, but print your letterhead yourself. Your printer can spit out single sheets as you need them—with the letter printed perfectly.

Once you've finished with your letterhead, you might want to design other documents that you'll be needing frequently. Figure 1 shows my most important document: my invoice. I created it with my word processor's "table" command, which lays out the format for me. For each new invoice, I replace the date, client name and address, and then just tab through the table, filling in the blanks for that client.

FIGURE 1   Sample Invoice

MILLENNIUM CONSULTING

1600 Pennsylvania Avenue
Washington, D.C. 20000-4541
(202) 555-1212
creative@getnet.com

January 5, 1997

Mr. Dick Clark
89 Dance to It Avenue
Beverly Hills, CA 90210

INVOICE FOR SERVICES RENDERED

Date	Description	Hours	Fee
1/1/97	Airbrushed live video feed to Internet to make you appear 25 again	3.5	$350.00
1/3/97– 1/4/97	Programmed Power Macintosh 99000 to simulate the late Ed McMahon for Publishers Clearing House Giveaway	22.00	$2,200.00
		Total:	$2,550.00
		Less received:	$1,000.00
		Amount due:	$1,550.00

The invoiced sum is due upon receipt of this bill. Please make checks payable to Millennium Consulting and mail to the above address. A late charge of 2% per month will be billed to invoices that are more than 30 days overdue.

If you have any questions, please feel free to call me at (202) 555-1212.

Sincerely,

Jeffry Porten

Jeff Porten

Over time it will become very clear which documents you'll be using repeatedly. There's the standard "nice to have met you" letter, the "thanks for the referral" letter, the "you asked me more about such-and-such service" letter, and the unforgettable "you still owe me money" letter. Business letters are a fantastic way to remind your clients and prospects that you exist, so have your computer set up to get these out quickly and conveniently.

A Word about Words

For some reason, the hardest language for most Americans isn't Spanish, French, or Urdu. It's business English. When forced to set pen to paper or fingertip to keyboard, all of a sudden "great to meet you" becomes "glad to have made your acquaintance."

It's true that for most business letters, even the style I'm using in this book won't fly. Too many apostrophes, and too many colloquialisms like "fly." But just because you're supposed to use the queen's English doesn't mean you have to switch to the heavy, laden, boring prose that they taught you in English class.

Crafting words is an art form, and doing it well will set you apart from the crowd and make your letters a pleasure to read. Writing poorly will mark you as a buffoon, frankly. If writing is not a natural gift for you, then take the time to learn how. The best one-book course I know is William Zinsser's *On Writing Well*.

Playing the Blue Cross Blues

One of the wonderful benefits of living in the United States is the freedom of having your life savings wiped out by catastrophic illness. While most other Western democracies think of health insurance as a basic prerequisite of citizenship, Americans basically sink or swim on their own.

Our age group still generally basks in our own immortality, so many of you have probably assumed that you could get by without insurance. That's what I did—after all, young, healthy people couldn't possibly have anything go wrong with them. Why waste the money?

Then I woke up one bright Friday morning in an ambulance. I realized I was in trouble when I had to figure out what year it was—that and a few other basic facts just weren't at my fingertips like they used to be. It seems I had collapsed while wandering through a hotel lobby on a business trip, managing to ricochet my head off the tiled floor in the process. A battery of tests later, my diagnosis was simple exhaustion. I had pushed myself so hard that I simply fell over where I stood.

Reassuring to hear, but it cost me nearly $3,000. That's money I would have saved if I had "wasted" a few bucks on insurance—and it's a fair bet that some assistance from an insurance provider might have put me on track to avoid exhaustion in the first place.

If you're employed by someone else, your best bet is to find out if you can get insurance through a COBRA extension of your existing insurance. Your benefits coordinator can point you in the right direction. Group health insurance is almost always more comprehensive and cheaper than anything you can land once you're on your own.

There are two kinds of health insurance: traditional plans and HMOs. A traditional plan takes your health history into account when you join, but it's easier to find a plan that you can get as an individual. Traditional plans cover your health costs after a yearly "deductible" has been paid. Even after that, though, your plan will generally only cover 80 percent of your costs. Once you've racked up enough costs, most plans will cover 100 percent of anything extra—but the catch is that they'll slap you with a cut-off point in the six or seven figures, after which you're on your own. Land yourself in the hospital for a long time and you might be in serious trouble.

Most traditional insurance plans provide you with a list of preferred providers (PPOs)—stick with their people and you'll get get more of your medical costs covered per visit. You can get traditional insurance plans with lower yearly deductibles, but then you'll be paying higher monthly premiums for the insurance.

The HMO plan is somewhat different. HMOs have very small payments for most doctor's visits, and you're not slapped with deductibles. HMOs also don't have caps, so a major accident or lingering illness won't land you into bankruptcy. However, you don't get preferred providers—you get required providers. Choose a doctor outside the network, and it's almost all out of your pocket. HMOs also require you to see a general practitioner and get his permission to see a specialist, and then the HMO organization has to approve the referral (which they often do—but this takes extra time). Note that gynecologists are considered to be "specialists" in this scenario.

Call around to a number of insurance providers to see what they're offering, or ask around at an entrepreneurial get-together. For the generally healthy, go with an HMO if you want to see doctors on a regular basis for wellness issues and basic prescriptions. If you'd rather stay away from medicine and just be covered for big-time problems, take out some traditional insurance with a high deductible.

Or you can roll the dice and look both ways before you cross the street. Hope it works out better for you than it did for me.

Acting Like a Good Capitalist Citizen

The only sure things in life are death and taxes. Time for you to deal with number two.

I n the current state of political affairs, I feel compelled to say a word or two in defense of taxes. It's awfully stylish these days to begrudge the government every dime they take out of our pockets and to insist that we live in a fascist society run by demonic greedheads who don't know how hard we work to make the money they take.

That to me is an incredibly cowardly view of money and our country. Taxes support the government that we have collectively built—a system that is more truly "of the people, by the people, for the people" than any other system of governance on the planet. If you don't like it, change it. Work to put your favorite people in positions of power, vote in every election, and contribute to important causes. Or shut up.

The debates over taxes are the result of too many whining people whose foremost question in their minds is, "What's in it for me?" Democracy requires that all its citizens consider, "What's in it for us?" Ignoring this responsibility in economic and political terms is the path to civic damnation.

Your first job is to make sure that all of your governments are copacetic with your business and won't come calling some day with a major fine and legal proceedings. Despite the joys of the free market, most municipalities require entrepreneurs to buy business permits before they start doing business. This is meant to prevent people from raising alligators for purses in their basements.

Check with your local government to find out what forms need to be filed. If you're doing business under a name that is not your own, you'll also need to file a fictitious-name registration. For a sole proprietorship, the fees should be nominal. If you're going to have employees, it gets more complicated—call an attorney or the SBA and have them help you through the process.

Kicked Off EZ Street

If you've been filing your taxes using the IRS's 1040EZ form, say good-bye. Entrepreneurs have to go with the full 1040, plus (horrors!) additional tax schedules. Lord knows why they call it a schedule since you have to file and pay at the same time as everyone else.

Entrepreneurial income goes onto Schedule C, which gets appended to your other tax forms. A box on the 1040 form needs to be filled in with the number from the last square on Schedule C, so you'll need them both to complete your taxes.

A copy of your Schedule C may also be required when you file your state and local taxes. State and local tax forms usually just ask you to file the key numbers off the 1040 form, so work out your federal taxes first, then pop on down to state and local.

If you've never done your own taxes before—I hadn't before I got out of grad school—don't panic, it's not that bad.

The IRS publishes a small booklet for every form, which details every line item on that form. The logic behind some of these instructions may seem beyond the grasp of mere citizens, but with a few hours and a shot of whiskey, the haze should start to lift.

Same Time, Next Quarter

Following the letter of the law, an entrepreneur is supposed to file his taxes quarterly, not annually. That is, you still do the big enchilada every April 15, but then every three months after that you're supposed to send in a check for your estimated taxes for that quarter. The logic behind this is that our employed brethren get their taxes deducted every paycheck, so we therefore have to do the same ourselves. (The logic behind both of these is that the government is smart enough to realize that no one is going to save one-third of their income all year to have it ready in April.)

The kicker is that the penalties on late quarterly payments (that is, paying it all in April) are usually pretty small. Your first year they probably won't even notice. Until you file your first Schedule C, they have no way of knowing that you're operating a business, and you have no prior year's income by which to estimate this coming year's taxes. That being said, the IRS has the power to play "gotcha" with you anytime you don't make a quarterly payment. Paying your quarterlies on time will save you hassle and money later.

Reporting Your Income

The IRS allows you to report your income by one of two methods: cash or accrual. On a cash basis, it doesn't matter when you make a sale or have an expense, only when the money is received or spent. On an accrual basis, the recording of the sale counts as the taxable date.

For most small businesses, cash-basis taxes are the simplest way to go, since most of us will be working on a cash basis anyway. The key for the entrepreneur isn't when the sale is made, but when the spending money comes in, so why pay taxes on sales not yet made?

The exception is when a business maintains an inventory. Since inventory-based businesses tend to move materials in and products out in advance of cash payments for purchases, the IRS automatically requires accounting on an accrual basis. If you're not certain where your business falls, consult the IRS, an accountant, or the SBA.

In the Poorhouse in April?

Many entrepreneurs are caught in a serious bind come April. Taxes are due, but their incomes have been barely enough to sustain them. Little money has been put into the fridge, let alone saved for the tax man. When the IRS comes knocking, there are a few obvious courses of action, including running like hell for the border.

As tempting as it may be, whatever else you do, don't skip filing your taxes. Period. If you file on time and you don't pay, you're merely a tax delinquent. If you don't file at all, you're a tax evader. The IRS has a funny way of putting tax evaders on forced vacations in taxpayer-supported facilities.

If taxes are a long way off as you read this, you can save yourself a major hassle by saving a chunk of your income. One benefit of working for yourself is that no one takes tax money out of your paychecks. Of course, that's also a drawback because you'll just have to pay it later. Put one-quarter to one-third of your income into a savings account or a three-month or six-month certificate of deposit, and forget about it until tax time. Then pay off your taxes and pocket the interest.

If taxes are looming and you have no bucks, file the forms and leave out the check. Don't bother writing a bad check—it'll do you no good and cost bank fees. In a few months the IRS will start sending you letters asking for their money. You can call them now or call them later. Call them later, and they will eventually send you certified mail informing you that if you don't pay, they will seize your assets. When that happens, it *would* be a good time to head for the border.

If all of this sounds like I have an intimate knowledge of the process, well, you got me. I called the feds before I got into serious trouble, and I was downright shocked at how polite and helpful they were. This truly is the kinder, gentler IRS. Save yourself the Maalox bills that I incurred and call them when they first inform you about the taxes due. Establishing good faith early on is a good idea, since you'll be working with them for some time to come.

CHAPTER 8

Full-Time Diets on Part-Time Incomes

*M*ost entrepreneurial guides start with a maxim that they say absolutely, positively, should not be violated: "start with at least six months' worth of living expenses stored in savings."

Now, this is good, sound advice. It's also poppycock. When I started out, I had about one month's worth of food, thanks to Mom and Dad stocking my pantry when they helped me move. Beyond that, I could set aside maybe 55¢, three raisins, and a Grape-Nut. Six months of expenses came out to more than $4,000—which, coincidentally, was pretty close to what I owed MasterCard thanks to my profligate graduate days.

If you have the good luck to be working in a secure job that provides you with lots of extra disposable income before you forge off on your own, and your business hits the big time early on, then you may never need the ideas in this chapter.

But for the other 90 percent, here are some ideas for putting money in your pocket and food on the table. I'll start with the obvious methods, then segue into more, ah, creative ideas.

One point that I cannot emphasize enough is that starting a business is hard, full-time, and frequently draining work. When you take on other work commitments for financial reasons, *they* must always be the part-time commitment, *not* your business. The country is filled with dreamers who work full-time and devote an hour here and there to writing a business plan or putting some ideas down on paper. These people are not entrepreneurs—they are novelists. If you don't want to fail before you begin, you *must* commit yourself to your ideas and make all other financial considerations and commitments secondary.

Temp Work—The Harpy of the 1990s

The rise of the temp worker is one of the symptoms of this crazy job market that leads many to entrepreneurship in the first place. Businesses shed workers left and right, cut expenses to the bone, and treat employees like "just-in-time" inventory: when we need you, show up. After that, stay home.

Now, thanks to all sorts of labor laws that we take for granted, businesses aren't allowed to treat real employees quite this poorly. So, the free market being what it is, they've developed legal mechanisms to exploit workers for just a little while and then send them packing.

I probably shouldn't sound so harsh—temping actually is a pretty sweet deal at first. You show up in a nicely appointed office with leather couches and computer magazines on the coffee tables. The receptionist offers you some coffee or candy—lemon Jolly Ranchers in my case—and then you're led in for the most painless job interview of your life. The interviewer makes it very clear that they *want* to hire you, that the bread and butter of their firm is to have as many people working as much as possible, and they'll truthfully tell you that the biggest problem of most temp firms isn't finding clients, but rather finding temps to work for their clients. These people are *thrilled* when you show up with skills they can use, and often those skills can be as paltry as typing reasonably well or knowing how to alphabetize and add without using your toes.

Best of all, we're talking some serious ready cash. Temp work usually pays between $7 and $15 an hour, sometimes much higher with the right skills. Many firms will place you the next morning, maybe even the same day if they're hungry enough for what you've got. Most glorious of all, there's that shining paycheck each week, which you walk off with even if the guy you're working for is a deadbeat. (If you're temping somewhere that doesn't pay you until *they* get paid, get the hell out of there.)

In return for all this, you get a job that's usually with a major company, with all the normal entry-level perks: microwave popcorn, coffee pots burbling away in the morning, air conditioning, and all the Bic disposable pens you can eat. If you're doing office temp work, there's usually no heavy lifting and no dirty work, except the odd Xerox toner replacement. The work is occasionally stressful, but we're not talking brain surgery.

And if you're working with a halfway decent temp firm, they'll give you a few bennies along with the cash, such as training classes, discounts at stores, freebie giveaways, and recognition in the newsletter when a client calls and says you're the greatest thing since the invention of toast. Most also have genuine job benefits, such as health insurance and paid vacation, after you've worked a certain number of hours within a year, usually 1,000. (This translates to twenty-five weeks of forty hours, or a half-year of full-time hours.)

Sounds great, doesn't it? It's the perfect way to make some cash on the side while you get your nascent business out of the fetal stage. Except for one thing.

Temp workers are Information Society bottom feeders.

The temp position is sold by the firms as the next best thing to entrepreneurship—set your own hours, choose your own work. In truth, that's not that case; the most valuable temps are the ones who are ready at a moment's notice—and *always* ready at a moment's notice. Turning down assignments is a great way to not get new ones.

When you agree to take a temp job, you're there to replace someone who's sick, or to fill in a temporary staffing hole on a project. Count on 99.9 percent of the people you work for to treat you like an idiot. There are two reasons for this, the first being that many temp workers actually *are* idiots, or at least reasonable facsimiles thereof. At my first temp job, fresh out of high school, I was the thirteenth person assigned, and the first one who could do the job: dividing paperwork into legal and correspondence, alphabetizing by last name. I would have guessed that any semi-evolved primate could have taken that job, as did my employers, but the pool of available talent, such as it was, proved them wrong.

The second, more important reason is that many temps are more competent than the people they work with. Unfortunately, it's the permanent people who have reputations to defend and posteriors to protect, and they're the ones who know how to play office politics. As a result, the credit for your good work will go to your supervisors, and you'll be left with the blame for their screw-ups.

So what, you say. After all, you're just in this for the money; let other people take the credit, so long as you can get the dinero you need to get your own venture running.

If you can sustain this attitude, more power to you. I could for awhile, but ultimately the pinheads wore me down. There are only so many times you can die the death of a thousand paper cuts before they ultimately get to you. It's hard to think of yourself as a resourceful, powerful entrepreneur when you've spent all day listening to a pinstriped Neanderthal tell you the proper way to hold a stapler.

Temp work is an excellent way to make contacts, and to see how the corporate game is played. If you have no experience with corporate America, I strongly recommend you get some, if for no other reason than to see how little a large company will think about spending obscene quantities of money for the product or service they need on deadline.

Temping is a good way to find a few mentors when you do land a good assignment—but there's a fine line between casually mentioning your entrepreneurial ventures and allowing them to supersede the temporary assignment you've been sent to do. This is especially the case when your entrepreneurial service overlaps in any way with the temporary services you are providing. Your temp firm will force you to sign a noncompetitive agreement when you start working for them. Violate this at great risk, both to your legal standing and your professional stature. On the other hand, read the agreement closely and ask for amendments when necessary. One firm I interviewed with basically asked me to say I would never work on a Macintosh in any major city in North America for three years. When they didn't take out that clause, I walked.

Remember also that temp work tends to take away prime business hours—much more so than some other lines of work. If your business idea requires phone calls or errand running between nine and five, make sure you take only short assignments or two-day-a-week stints; if you work five days, you'll have to put your plans on hold. If your dreams aren't worth more to you than cash, you've got no business being in business.

Schlepping Food

It sometimes seems like waiting tables is the Great American Occupation of our generation. Again, there are some pretty nice features to this line of work: cash in hand at the end of the day, a variety of workplaces to choose from, and if you like chatting with people and providing customer service, you sure as hell get your opportunities. Many places will toss in a free or reduced-cost meal as part of the bargain.

That having been said, waiting tables is hard work. I've never done it, but I've never known anyone who did and came home ready for anything other than an easy night out or a quiet evening in. This also just might be the only profession in which the workers are treated worse than temps. Check with friends who have already tried this, and make sure you're not in one of those cities notorious for bad tips before you get yourself snared.

Rent Your Body to Science

Did you ever read in the paper about new decongestants that were 95 percent effective, but that caused some weird side effect—like male pregnancy—in the other 5 percent? Here's your chance to be one of those lucky 5 percent.

The nation's pharmaceutical companies have money to spend on guinea pigs. Those guinea pigs must be humans, since by the time they get to human trials all the real guinea pigs are dead, along with a large number of rats, bunny rabbits, and chimpanzees. So what they do is round up a bunch of healthy human beings, fortify them with money and oddball instructions, and give them experimental drugs to see if anyone gets sick.

If you're not quite ready for that, an easier way to make money by legal body-part prostitution is to sell your blood. Despite blood drives and the work of the Red Cross, there is still a desperate need for certain blood types, especially O, the "universal donor" type, and negative Rh types. (If you don't know your type, they'll tell you at your first donation.) Most drives will give away donuts or small sandwiches to donors, so you might be able to get a meal out of it—but if you shop around, you can probably find a drive that pays $15 or $20 a pint.

Don't donate more often than once every two months or so. Some folks have been known to give fake names and donate as often as once a week, which is downright stupid. Your body will replace the blood-fluid volume within twenty-four hours or so, but it takes longer to replace the cellular matter that makes blood a life fluid. Overdonating is a fast way to turn yourself into a human zombie.

And it should go without saying, but for God's sake, if you may be at risk for HIV or hepatitis B or some other blood-borne disease, don't even *think* about donating. Some people have donated infected blood figuring that the screening process will prevent it from being circulated, and that by then they'll be far gone with their cash. The problem is that screening is not 100 percent effective, thanks to bureaucratic inefficiencies. At best, a tainted unit may require the disposal of thousands of units of blood; at worst, someone else may be infected. Don't risk the possibility of this happening.

If you want to get into slightly higher blood stakes, find a university research unit that works with blood. Their requirements are a lot stricter, so the pay is better. When I was an undergrad, the going rate for a pint was $15, but I found a lab that was willing to pay $40 for ten ounces of platelet-rich blood, which I just happen to have.

For guys, most major cities have programs that pay very good money for certain other bodily fluids. Yeah, you know what I'm talking about. This usually involves an initial visit where you'll be tested to see if your sperm count is high enough; after that, you can visit every few days and make $50 a, er, pop. Sometimes the sperm is used for genetic research, but more frequently it's for artificial insemination. Keep in mind that, by law, you as the donor will never be told whether your materials were used for a successful insemination. I wasn't comfortable with the idea of not knowing if I had genetic offspring wandering around somewhere, so I never went through with this—but it's good money (and a good service to childless couples) if that doesn't bother you. The other downside is that these programs require you to remain totally celibate during your participation.

So, after blood and semen, what's next? Well, the big money is in experimentation, and—as you might guess—the more invasive or painful the procedure, the more bucks in your pocket. Here's a crash course in modern medicine from the guinea pig's point of view.

New medicines, drugs, and treatments must go through years of clinical trials before they are allowed to be sold to or used on the everyday patient. Most are tested on three criteria: safety, effectiveness, and side effects. Before they're tested on human subjects, however, hundreds of tests are performed on laboratory animals: first on rats, which are physiologically remarkably similar to humans (and vice versa in some cases), and then on up through the evolutionary chain to higher primates. By the time humans are tested, the researchers are fairly certain about what the effects will be, but there is no way of knowing for sure until the trials are run.

The important thing to know is that drug trials won't kill you; when you hear of humans dying in trials, it's usually people who were sick with a disease that only the trial drug could cure, and who took the risk in an attempt to get well. There are cases of clinical drugs causing side effects or discomforts that are far worse than anticipated, which is about the worst you can expect. The scientists running the trials are required by law to tell you everything that might possibly happen to you, but you still have to learn to read between the lines to make sure that you know what is going to happen.

The best studies to get into involve sleep deprivation, in my opinion. If you're a student or recently graduated, it's probably nothing worse than what you do to yourself on a regular basis, and your daytime hours will be left free to get some work done if you're still mentally competent. The study I participated in consisted of two sessions in the hospital, four days each; on days one and four I was wired to the EKG machines and allowed to sleep normally; on days two and three my REM sleep was interrupted. I slept off the effects after the research, $800 richer.

Some other experiments are slightly hairier. I interviewed for the following, all of which I was accepted for but turned down. The first involved radioactive iodine and a nuclear magnetic resonance imaging session, for $500. At the time I was working in a lab that used radioactivity, so I didn't want the additional risk. The second was an $800 removal of hip bone marrow. It sounded great until a med school friend of mine told me that the "discomfort" involved would last three months or so, as this was one of the most painful procedures around. If you're going to do this, it pays to have friends in med school.

The last one I considered was a cholera study, where first they would have given me an experimental vaccine, then a dose of cholera, and watched to see if I got sick. If I did, they would have cured me immediately, so at most I'd be in for a few days of severe discomfort. In return, I'd spend a week in an entertainment center with the other participants, and get a check for $1,000 after it was all done. Then I read the fine print: two months later they would run the experiment again, but this time they wanted a control group—people who would get the cholera dose with *no* vaccine.

If you still think this is for you, check the volunteer sections of the classified ads in the weekly Health section of your major daily newspaper, or in the classifieds of local college newspapers. Make sure that volunteers will be compensated, as many studies are done with no money attached.

Barter

This can be one of the best ways of keeping yourself afloat: trade your service or product for food. This has the great advantage of actually being in your line of work, and if you haven't officially started your business yet, it'll be great practice. Of course, bartering will involve some of the same marketing dilemmas as finding cash-paying customers. How do you find people willing to trade what they have for what you have? In this case, however, it'll be much easier, since you'll start by identifying the people who have the resources you need. It might be the owner of a local grocery, or a nearby restaurant, or a dry cleaner, or even an apartment building or office complex. Even if many of these people would be hard to get as customers, it is often less difficult to arrange a trade, especially if they have something that they can't sell, or that might be costing them money, such as excess inventory.

When I started out, I often traded Macintosh consulting in return for a home-cooked meal; it was (and still is) a standing offer to any of my friends or networking acquaintances who needed more information from me than I could easily relay in a few minutes. Not only did this solve the immediate problem of finding nourishment, but it also solidified the opinions of many people that I was a top-notch consultant. And while none of these people has ever called me back and offered to hire me for cash, their bosses and contacts have. Often.

Which leads me to Rule One of barter: *never* provide shoddy goods or services to a client or customer because they are not paying you cash. This is a corollary to the rule that you should never provide shoddy goods or services, period. But the temptation is often great to pass off poorly made goods or half-assed services because, after all, you're not *really* getting compensated for your work. This is an unprofessional attitude, and it will come back to haunt you later. (Of course, you can sometimes barter unsellable goods if the customer is fully aware of the defects; this is an excellent method of turning lemons into lemonade.)

Rule Two: evaluate your goods and services at their full retail value, and expect—no, *demand*—your customer to do the same. Again, this is one of the pernicious aspects of a no-cash transaction, the drive to look for a cut-rate deal. Don't trade your value-added products at the cost of materials, and don't ask your customer to do so either. Likewise, if you sell a service, set the value of that service at what you would charge in cash, even if you have no cash-paying clients. This is also an issue of professionalism, and it will reflect badly on your ethic if you try to pull a fast one.

On the flip side, don't count your barter services down to the penny. One of my most valuable networking contacts is the publisher of a local community newsletter, who also co-ordinates a home-business networking group. I provided him with a large project at low cost and ongoing consulting, in return for a monthly ad in his newsletter. I have no idea how many hundreds of hours of work I've given him, or if the value of my time is greater or less than what he would have billed me for the advertising—which is moot, since I wouldn't have been able to pay him cash. However, the data-base I designed has saved him tens of thousands of dollars in staff costs as he has been able to remain a one-man opera-tion. On my end, somewhere between 60 and 70 percent of my clients have resulted from those ads or from referrals by him—so neither of us is counting dollars. I've occasionally had cash-paying prospects mention the idea of barter to me when it is damn clear they can afford cash and I'd much rather have the money in my pocket. This was ticklish at first. The last thing you want is a client who feels like he or she is getting screwed out of some money. Their approach was usu-ally, "You know, Laura, who told me about your services, mentioned that you worked with her for two hours in return for a big pot of chili." The best response, I've found, is some-thing along the lines of, "Laura's a friend of mine who I fre-quently socialize with; my relationship with you is more professionally oriented. However, after we conclude these services at my usual rate, if you would like, I can spare some time for a casual working dinner at Café Boeuf, for which I will not charge you if you pick up the check." If you bill by the hour, most of the time you *do* charge for lunch and dinner meetings, but it's a good way of defusing a bad situation.

If you want to take the barter idea to a higher level, there are organizations that can help. These groups sign up hundreds of businesses that trade services for barter-dollars amongst themselves.

Theoretically, the IRS is more than willing to tack on taxes to income that you generate in bartered goods and services. So long as you keep it as a low-key addition to your cash-generating work, you should easily escape official notice. However, if a large portion of your living expenses are supported by barter, you should declare barter income. The barter associations can help you with this, or you can consult an accountant (bartering for her fees, naturally!).

Secrets to Cheap Eats

Even if the money you're bringing in is paltry, there are still ways to go to bed full, if not particularly nourished. Here are a few that kept me going:

- *Clipping Coupons.* It's boring and pedestrian, but it keeps the cupboards full. Clip every coupon for any product you can possibly see yourself eating, and then check the Sunday supplements and food sections of your local newspapers to find out what the supermarkets have on sale. Between double-coupons and half-off sales, you should be able to snag a few items each week for free. My own personal record was $35 worth of food for $7—a combination of buy-one, get-one-free cereals, coupons, and rebate offers. Coupon clipping usually works out to about $8 saved per hour of clipping and organizing, so it's not a great way to save money, but if you're not going to make money during that time anyway, why not go for it? Non-sugared cereals, pastas, and breads make for good, cheap bulk.

- *Happy Hours.* A local pizza joint offered half-price appetizers, free pizza, and free refills on soda during the first year I was in Washington. I went there about four times a week. A few slices of pizza, an order of garlic bread or a small salad, and a few liters of Diet Pepsi came out to $4.06. Not bad for a daily food budget.

- *Free Lectures and Events.* Many campuses and private bookish-type businesses sponsor talks by various distinguished guests. Don't worry about the topic—just look for the magic words "refreshments served."

- *Closeouts.* My local coffee shop sells pastries and bagels at half-price fifteen minutes before closing. A few times the counter attendant just gave me a free bag stuffed with goodies, since she was going to throw them out anyway. Pizza shops are a good place to check immediately before closing too, for leftover slices and other food that would otherwise be wasted.

If meals like this are going to be your diet for a while, splurge $2 on a bottle of multivitamins. A few cents a day can keep you from withering away until your diet can better supply your body's intake needs.

One nice thing about hunger: it's a real inspiration to start being more successful.

CHAPTER 9

Marketing Is *Not* Advertising

*Y*ou've got a product, you've got a location, you've got debts. All you need now are customers.

This is simultaneously the hardest and the funnest part of running a business. Marketing means creating a public image for your venture—letting people know who you are, what you do, and why they should hand you their cash. If you have even a smidgen of ego—and all entrepreneurs do— building up your business is the same as building up yourself. That's what makes it fun.

Many entrepreneurs mistakenly believe that marketing is a matter of money—buying television ads, blowing a chunk on the Yellow Pages listing, designing insanely expensive glossy brochures. You can certainly sink plenty of money into these things if you like, but there's no point to it. You'd be better off living within your budget and coming up with marketing ideas that are well-suited for your business and your personality.

Goudrix Productions is a perfect example of a company that knows how to market its stuff. I met the owners on a business trip in Avignon, France. I was in my usual spot at an outdoor café, satisfying my caffeine addiction, when I noticed them in the center of the public square. They were hard to miss. One of them was juggling a large tasseled stick with what looked like a pair of drumsticks. While he was twirling it around his head and throwing it up to ten feet into the air, two other guys were drinking beer and talking with a small crowd of young blondes.

This seemed like a fun job, so I headed over to ask them about it, and maybe chat with some of the blondes in the process. It turned out that the three of them were Quebecois natives who had started their own business manufacturing those large tasseled sticks. The stick was perfectly balanced, covered with cotton, and tipped with leather strips. Their usual marketing method was to head out in public, show off their skills with the stick—which frequently appeared to defy gravity—and sell as many as they could. Drinking and carousing also appeared to be a major part of their business plan.

They called their product the Flowerstick. It cost them about $6 each to produce, and they sold it for about $20 a pop. The packaging was very simple: a long, clear plastic bag contained the Flowerstick, the drumsticks, and a small card with instructions on how to juggle printed in English and French; the bag was stapled shut with a small piece of cardboard with their company logo on it.

All three were in their low- to mid-twenties, and were making more than enough money to finance their trip to France, Switzerland, and England. Meanwhile, back in Quebec they had fourteen employees—average age, twenty-one—making new sticks.

The Flowerstick and its marketing gave them a good life and a great living. Since starting the company, they had sold 40,000 Flowersticks, which by my calculations amounted to better than a half-million dollars in profit.

For people who weren't into sticks, they also sold Diablos for the same price. A Diablo looks like a rubber ball that has been cut in half and rejoined to form an hourglass shape. You juggle it by spinning it on a string tied to two sticks, after which you can toss it in the air and make the same sort of spectacle of yourself that you can with the Flowerstick. As another unique juggling toy, it gave Goudrix Productions a perfect product diversification. All they did was trade Flower-sticks for Diablos with a California company—a neat arrangement that cost them little money, added no complexity to their operation, and increased their sales.

Marketing *your* products may not be quite as fun, but there's no reason you can't use as much creativity as the Goudrix partners did.

Sell, Baby, Sell!

Remember in the business plan when we listed about a thousand ways to spend money and only three or four ways to make money? There's a reason for that: of all the activities you can undertake for your business, only sales will result in income. Everything else you do, morning, noon, and night, will be an expense in terms of either time or money. If you don't concentrate on sales, you're going to hemorrhage cash.

So your first task is to make sure that what you're selling is attractive to the buyer. We've already talked about pricing, so I'll assume that your prices and other product features make you competitive in your market. But now, try to think of other things you can do from a marketing standpoint to sacrifice a little money in return for a guaranteed sale. Here are some examples of what I'm talking about:

- *The Money-Back Guarantee.* This is fairly simple: offer a no-questions-asked return policy for your goods, and pay back in cash, not store credit. If you really want to move product, offer a 110 percent money-back guarantee—but make sure that no customer nails you more than once. If there's no risk for the consumer, there's a better chance they'll buy your product.

- *The Loss Leader.* When I was billing my clients at $40 an hour, I offered a first-time four-hour session for $100. The idea was that in four hours I would come away with a fairly long list of future work projects that I could suggest, while the client was picking up my time at a discount. I found out over time that I didn't need to do this. My clients had very little price resistance, so there was no need to offer low-cost sessions. But at the time, it increased my bottom line tremendously.

- *Shared Profits.* One of the services I offer is essentially the formation of another product, which the client and I then market jointly. I charge my clients a flat fee for my work, but then I let them keep all the profits that come in until they've made back my fee. After that, we split the profits. So my clients know that, at worst, they'll be charged a few thousand dollars. If the project goes well, however, they may make a profit on my services—and I'll make that same profit, plus their original fee. Most clients I've proposed it to have found it awfully hard to turn down that offer.

What Are Your Customers Buying?

Always keep in mind the reasons your customers patronize you. Customers don't buy your goods and services for the good or service itself, but rather for its benefits. My clients don't pay me $75 an hour because they're lonely; they pay me that so they can work more efficiently long after I've gone home.

If you're selling a winter coat, you'll want to emphasize the benefits of the coat, not the coat itself. Unless you're Bill Blass, no one cares that your name is on the label. But they do want it to be warm when they wear it in snowdrifts, and they definitely don't want to look like a total dork when they go out in public. So advertise that it's made of a revolutionary fabric that keeps them toasty (assuming that's true, of course), without giving them that hairy land-whale look that everyone gets when they wear a fur coat.

Targeting Your Market

Who are the people who will be buying from you? You can't expect to sell baby diapers to a senior citizens' community. You have to decide which of the five-odd billion people on the planet will be your customers, and why. Then you start convincing them of this fact.

Come up with as many ways as you can think of to cate-
gorize the people who might be your market: where they
live, who they live with, what they wear, how old they are, how
old they look and feel, the work they do, the hobbies they
enjoy, and on and on. Determine which cross sections will be
interested in buying what you're selling.

When I was in high school, a bunch of us showed up every
morning at 7 A.M. with drug paraphernalia. The reason was
that we all played wind instruments, and the same cigarette
papers commonly used to wrap joints also made fine blotting
papers for the spit that inevitably came pouring out of our instruments. Just the right size, just the right absorbency.

If the head shop down the street ever got wind of this,
they might have come up with a whole new marketing strategy. First, repackage reefer paper as a primo spit blotter.
Second, give out free samples at youth orchestra concerts.
Third, send letters to school principals letting them know
the legitimate use for this product, and why they shouldn't
bust students who get caught with it.

Sounds crazy, but it's true. Most products and services
can find markets far afield of where they started. My mother
uses Krazy Glue on her fingernails to make them hard as
Sheetrock, and to date she hasn't permanently attached herself to the kitchen table. A popular hand lotion does a better
job of keeping mosquitoes away than the actual bugs-away
products. And a company that makes horse shampoo is now
selling a large fraction of its product to humans who use it
for their own hair.

Keep your eyes open for uses of your product or service
that might not seem obvious at first. Encourage sales in new
markets by looking for other businesses and industries that
might have some overlap with yours. Learn as much as you

can about other markets—the more you know, the more connections you will find.

Small Is Beautiful

Believe it or not, your size is a key advantage in marketing. Unlike those lumbering, behemoth corporations, you don't have the luxury of multimillion-dollar budgets, but you also don't have to get the approval of twenty vice-presidents before you can make a move. Come up with an idea in the morning, and you can have it out in front of the public in the afternoon.

That sort of speed is your real edge. Entrepreneurs are out in the streets, ready to pounce on new markets that the big boys don't even know exist. It's your job to find them and land clients, so by the time the big guns roll into town, you've got customer loyalty to keep them coming back. Never mind the fact that you'll also be competing against other small businesses. Stay one step ahead of them with fast action and smart analysis, or get eaten for lunch.

Fast Marketing Still Pays Off Slowly

Every form of marketing, from million-dollar TV buys to showing up at a business gathering with a few cards, is an investment of time and money. Like most investments, these pay off very slow dividends that might not be visible for a long time to come. I don't go to a business luncheon with the expectation of coming home with a check, a new client, or even a vague commitment for future services. I expect to come home with a few names and numbers, and some requests for more information. My follow-through on those is yet another investment—and if I miss that chance by not writing or calling, then I've wasted my original time and money.

Marketing is an incremental process: slowly, over time, people start to recognize who you are and what you do. Even then, they may not be ready to hand you money; that takes the building of more trust. In the meantime, you'll be making an income from the few who are willing to go with first impressions and write checks quickly. But the long haul is when you'll really see the marketing pay off.

Make a Consistent Effort

Showing up on people's radar once every eight weeks probably isn't good enough. You want your prospects to instantly make a connection between who you are and what they need. That requires persistence to overcome their natural tendency to forget who you are. The best way to stick in people's minds is to be there, time and again, whenever they're looking.

I don't attend every weekly meeting of one of my networking groups, but I'm there at least half the time. And I showed up _every_ time for the first year, getting to know the organizers and the founders of the group, and turning some of them into clients. Now, I'm well enough known by the regulars that I'll frequently get calls from new clients when I _don't_ show up because others there were talking about me.

Your marketing, whether in person or in print, must inspire confidence in your business as a rock-solid source of help. All you have to do to create that confidence is be there.

Choosing the Right Media

There are as many ways to get out your message as there are businesses. The key to choosing the right ones is to consider your budget and your products.

Take as an example late-night television, which is the cheapest way to advertise on the tube. That's a good place to be if you're selling a dating service, based on the demographics of who watches television at two in the morning. But it wouldn't be appropriate for a grocery store that doesn't open until 10 A.M.

Likewise, the advertising space in the local rooms-for-rent circular might be very cheap, but it wouldn't generate much business for a house-painting service.

Always consider first the media that costs you the least, and work your way up to the more expensive commitments. Showing up at meetings and trade shows with brochures and flyers will cost only a little time and money. Milk those opportunities for all they're worth before moving on to placing advertisements.

With both advertisements and printed materials, consider carefully who you're trying to reach, and which benefits of your products or services will appeal the most to them. It's perfectly fine to emphasize one set of appeals to one market, and a very different set to another. Just keep your costs low. You'd be far better off running a few ads for a long time than running many for a short time because you can't afford to keep them going.

Marketing Your Business by Marketing Yourself

The sum total of marketing I've done has consisted of a single print ad in a community newsletter, and networking like a banshee. Total cost: $0 for the print ad thanks to the barter arrangement, and a few bucks a week for what I consume at the meetings. Most of my business has come through word-of-mouth advertising.

I make a point of knowing a lot of people. My credo is "show up." I'll give most networking groups at least one try, and I'm always ready to chat up my services with random passersby. I might find a prospect during a ride on a train, a plane, or even an elevator. (I've tried escalators—too awkward.)

An excellent method of marketing is to make yourself a walking billboard. Just go where you might find your next customer, and have your product with you or information that you can spread around. And if one particular group of people doesn't bite, find yourself another. And another.

I'm a member of three networking groups that meet either weekly or monthly. I'm also a founder of a fourth group, the Noodle Club, where I indulge a passion for activism and make business contacts as I go. Founding a networking group can be difficult—by definition, you'll need a lot of contacts to get it off the ground—but if it takes off, you'll be in the catbird seat as organizer and head honcho. (If you're curious about my group, you'll find more information about it in appendix D.)

Your Time Is Valuable—Barter It!

Try finding organizations that would benefit from your expertise, and approach them about giving free speeches or presentations. Give a short speech about something topical that's of interest to the audience, and make it clear that this is only a taste of the benefits that could be had if they hired you or bought your product. A speech should not be an infomercial, but it should also not leave the audience guessing what you do for a living or why you're there.

Teaching puts you in a position of authority. Get in front of a room of people, and they will listen to what you have to say. Be of any use at all to them, and your business will have cleared several hurdles to landing them as clients.

Use Your Customers for Cheap Marketing

The best way to turn the teeming masses into Mongol hordes invading your shop to throw money at you is to get at their hearts and minds one by one. They'll be resistant to anything you say—after all, you're the maker of the product, so of course you're biased—but they'll probably be very interested in the opinions of their best friends or mothers-in-law, who might already be customers of yours.

Encourage your existing customers to bring in new ones. You might not have to do anything more than ask if they know anyone who might need your product. Most people, once they've found something they like, get satisfaction out of recommending it to others. You can leech off this goodwill impulse without spending a dime. Just ask your customers on a regular basis to bring in a friend. Or, for service businesses, just hand out extra business cards to clients who mention that they know people interested in your service.

Ask your clients to make the initial contact, and then have the new prospect give you a call so you can clinch the sale.

Or you can put your money where your mouth is. Give existing clients a discount when they bring in new customers. Give clients who bring you referrals gift certificates to local stores or restaurants. Come up with a consistent system to remind your customers to look for new clients for you, and reward them when they do it.

Remember, though, don't kill the golden goose. Referrals come primarily through goodwill. If your incentive starts seeming more like a bribe, you'll turn off your clients, and your new referrals will drop in quality.

Stay on Your Prospect's Radar

All right, you've collected a few hundred business cards, and they're all in some sort of Rolodex. You've been taking notes about who's in what business, and you know who said "maybe next month" and who said "I like your service, but we're not in the market."

Over time, you'll develop a feel for which prospects will be good leads and which ones are cold as ice. It's a tricky thing to learn. Sometimes a prospect will be distant in person, and you'll be just about to write them off when they drop a sale in your lap. Other prospects make it seem that they're so hot for your service, they'll have a check in your hand tomorrow—and then string you along for months. Look for the nuances that tell you what's really going on. A prospect who's constantly getting permission from "others" in his company is a cold lead. People who talk the talk without having anything to back it up will usually slip up somewhere along the line, making nervous gestures and speaking in hesitant phrases. Watch for these miscues and read between the lines of what they're telling you.

Regardless, leads are leads, and it's worth following up on all of them until you're confident in your ability to accurately judge their worth. Only rarely will a prospect call you out of the blue. In most cases, you'll have to ask for a sale to get one. The best way to do this is usually the simplest: through the U.S. Postal Service or by telephone. Make a master list of all your leads, and be sure to contact them monthly or bimonthly. A short newsletter with useful information is a great way of doing this; if they hear from you on a regular basis, they'll think about you on a regular basis.

I write a bimonthly newsletter that I send to my best prospects. (See figure 1.) I keep my newsletters to four pages or less so I can fit them on one double-sided eleven-by-seventeen sheet of paper; folded over, it makes a four-page newsletter. The bottom of page four leaves space for the client's address; the "Inside This Millennium Journal" section is the first thing he reads before he opens the stapled letter, which is usually two or four pages. I fold it into thirds and put the client's mailing label and my return address on the bottom third of the last page. The middle third has a summary of what they'll find inside, so clients who usually don't open junk mail will at least see what I have to say before they decide whether to throw it out. By using the last page of the newsletter as the outside of the letter, I'm creating what's called a self-mailer—no envelope costs or time spent stuffing them.

You can buy mailing lists from marketing services, but these usually cost an arm and a leg. Better to build your own: meet many people, get them into your database, then contact them. Ask for referrals; collectively, your contacts know more people than you do. Follow up mailings with phone calls, which should go as follows: "Did you get my letter? What did you think? Do you have any questions?" Regular contact is the key to regular sales.

THE MILLENNIUM JOURNAL

SEPTEMBER 1995

PUBLISHED BY MILLENNIUM CONSULTING

Contents

The Millennium Journal is a publica-tion of Millennium Consulting. Neither Millennium Consulting nor The Millennium Journal is affiliated with any other organization in Washington, D.C., or elsewhere.

Millennium Consulting pro-vides training, seminars, cus-tom software, and consulting on the productive use of Macintosh computers, the Internet, World Wide Web publishing, and other information technologies. We specialize in small business, home office, and non-profit clients.

Please note our new address:
**1600 Pennsylvania Ave., NW
Washington, D.C.
20008-4541
(202) 555-1212
creative@getnet.com**

WINDOWS 95 CATCHES UP WITH MACINTOSH 1988

Now that the release date of Microsoft Windows 95 has come and gone, per-haps we might be spared the marketing blitz that has inundated the computer world. For Macintosh users, it's been pretty tiresome. After all, the brave new world that Windows 95 gives IBM users is the same one we've been comfortably living in for years.

Let's take a look at some of the great new features of Windows 95. The con-venient new "Start" menu, which dupli-cates the Apple menu we've been using. The "recycling bin," which was proba-bly not named "Trash" to avoid yet an-other Apple lawsuit. (And Apple lets us change our minds and take things back out of the trash—not so in Win95.) The ability to do several things at once? We've had that since System 6.

Windows 95 is great news for that small subset of IBM users who have a recent, powerful computer, and several hundred disposable dollars to spend on new software. Don't be fooled by the low price of Win95; upgraders will also have to buy new versions of their other software. According to the catalog I have here, that'll run them $90 for Win95, $325 for the new Microsoft Office, and $50 for more software (the "Plus Pack") that wasn't included with Windows, including Internet con-nectivity.

All this for a computer that is almost, but not quite, as easy to use and cus-tomize as a Macintosh.

As best as I can tell, the only reason why IBMs dominate the market… is because IBMs dominate the market. De-spite Apple technology that would let them get more work done, better, faster, and cheaper.

If you're worried about missing out, here's all you're missing, quoted from a software technician in the *Wash-ington Post*: "I'd hate to be someone who doesn't know much about com-puters using this. For people who aren't technically inclined, if Windows 95 doesn't find their devices, they're in for a haul."

Studies show that people using Macs turn out higher quality work in less time. Macintosh can now convert files from any IBM to Mac and back again, and even run IBM programs, so compatibility is not an issue when you're forced to share work with the less fortunate.

When people have asked me in the past, I've told them the only reason to go IBM is if they've had a previous time investment learning Windows 3.1. With the advent of Win95, even that reason is now moot. For new and old users alike, the way to go is Macintosh.

MILLENNIUM MAC & INTERNET SEMINARS

Millennium is considering starting a seminar series on various aspects of Macintosh and Internet use. We want to know more about what you would like to see in terms of courses of-fered and the best logistical arrangements. Right now we're considering courses on the fol-lowing topics, offered on Saturdays and Sundays in the morning or afternoon, somewhere near the Cleveland Park metro. Courses would be four hours in length with a half-hour break in the middle. We want to hear from you to know if these are what you want—and if not, how can we change them to serve you better? Please call us with your ideas at (202) 555-1212.

Getting the Most Out of Your Mac

• Using System 7.0 and 7.5, networking, keyboard, and memory tricks to speed up your Mac and your work.

Microsoft Word 5.1 and 6.0.1

• The most powerful and least used com-mands of both, and which version to use to best suit your work.

Road Warrior 101

• PowerBooks, cell phones, pager—putting it all together to improve your business and ease your life.

The Internet and Online Services

• How to get online, where to go, what to do—making it useful and productive for business and personal use.

Inside This Millennium Journal:

• Windows 95 Hype and Hoopla—Mac's Been There, Done That
• Blowing the Doors Off Pentiums with the New Power Macs
• New Apple Software to Jazz Up Your Printing and Your Reality
• Double Your Pleasure with Doubling Software
• Macintosh and Internet Seminars

MILLENNIUM CONSULTING

1600 Pennsylvania Ave., NW
Washington, D.C. 20008-4541

And once you have the newsletter written, take copies with you whenever you go out on business. Be sure to staple business cards inside the newsletter and get more names every time you set foot out the door.

Going Ape over Guerrilla Marketing

If you're looking for more ideas on how to market, there's a great place to go for one-stop shopping. It's a series of books by Jay Conrad Levinson: *Guerrilla Marketing, Guerrilla Marketing Attack,* and *Guerrilla Marketing Excellence.* At least one of these books should be on your bookshelf. Guerrilla marketing is all about making major sales on small budgets, about finding the key methods of winning over prospects and customers. Levinson's books are filled with valuable information. I guarantee you'll miss sales if you don't follow his advice.

CHAPTER 10

The Care
and Feeding
of Chutzpah

I love Yiddish. After thousands of years of persecution, the Jews have come up with a language in which every word is rich in sarcasm and humor. Yiddish terms frequently don't translate directly into English. You can call someone a jerk, but it doesn't have the same style and richness of meaning as saying, with your voice dripping with contempt, that so-and-so is a real putz.

Chutzpah is the same kind of term. It's a word with equal parts arrogance, panache, bullheadedness, and confidence in the ability to get one's way, all thrown into a linguistic food processor and served warm with a side of courage and self-will.

The classic definition of chutzpah is the kid who murders his parents and then throws himself on the mercy of the court because he's an orphan. This was funnier in the days before the Menendez trial. Perhaps a better definition is any entrepreneur—someone with the nerve to say that she can create something out of her own mind, will, and work, for which other people will hand over their money regardless of the tens of thousands of other things they could spend their cash on.

Anyone starting a business already has a dose of chutzpah. It's much easier to nurture in those with a small amount than it is to grow in someone who's never had any. You can rest assured that you're at least a little chutzpahdik (i.e., laden with it) since you're reading this book. Now you're going to bring that part of your personality out in the force required to be successful at your business.

Aggressive, Yes! Confrontational, No!

Chutzpah usually walks the fine line between self-confidence and arrogance. Occasionally, it blows right past that and walks the fine line between arrogance and offensiveness. The proper application of chutzpah is understanding when to walk one line and when to walk the other.

Arrogance is a barrel of nuclear energy that you keep tightly stored in the recesses of your soul. Every entrepreneur should have some. The barrel will burn anything that comes in contact with it, and the heat it gives off warms your spirit from the inside out. Ninety-nine percent of the time you leave that barrel shut and let its warmth flow out of your personality. That warmth is self-confidence.

The core of my nuclear fires is the following equation: I am Jeff Porten. This resonates with the intonations with which one would say, "I am unique, I can work miracles, I have a heaping portion of the godhead at the core of my being." It's the absolute assurance that I am powerful enough and creative enough to handle whatever comes my way, to transmute the elements, to spin silk from sows' ears.

Were I to open this drum and let it become the core of my public persona, I would rapidly repulse everyone who comes in contact with me. My girlfriend is a saint for putting up with those brief times when my barrel does reach critical mass. No one who lets their barrel burn out of control will ever be able to maintain a friendship or relationship for any length of time, and their professional contacts will relish meetings with them like bouts of the plague.

As a result, I leaven my self-confidence with a healthy dose of self-deprecating humor. I recognize my faults, and I'm generally willing to call attention to them. Still, many people who come in contact with me and get a full dose of my confidence without that dash of humor come away with a negative impression. I've long since learned that that's the price of personality.

Arrogance is never having to say you're sorry. Chutzpah is apologizing abjectly when the situation calls for it, but when some people don't like you simply because you're strong-willed—well, that's *their* problem.

Start your nuclear reactors with the understanding—the deep, core belief—that you are *you*. That qualifies you to be uniquely suited for the work you've chosen, it gives you insights that no one else has, and it predisposes you for success.

Being you will not give you the ability to fly effortlessly over thousand-foot cliffs—the slings and arrows of mortal fortune hit us all, and more so the risk-takers—but it will give you the strength to scale that cliff with only a rope and three ounces of Gatorade.

Chutzpah in Action

You're at a business mingle, and people are wandering around looking for new contacts and new sales. Without chutzpah, you're just a face in the crowd. With it, everyone is there for the sole purpose of meeting you—you just have to make them aware of this.

If you don't have the self-confidence to pull this off, do not try to fake it. Let this meeting pass as a standard gathering with only a few contacts made, until the next time when your fires are burning brighter. Everyone has up and down days, and I've shown up at networking sessions too tired to let my chutzpah come to the fore. Sometimes, though, it surprises me, sneaking up during a conversation with prospect number one, and energizing me enough to meet prospects two through twenty.

Here's the chutzpahdik networking style:

Greeting

When you meet someone, you're warm and friendly. During the time you're talking to this person, he's not there to meet you, but the other way around, and you let it show with your mannerisms and words. Say "it's great to meet you," and really mean it.

If this is your first time meeting this person, ask for his name and really listen to the response. Names are forgotten because people are thinking about question number two when they should be listening. At a meeting of a thirty or even a hundred people, not having to ask someone their name twice is a real point in your favor. It's impossible to make someone feel unique when their name is Tom and you call him Dick or Harry.

If you've met the person before and his face doesn't call forth his name from your memory, preempt embarrassment: "Hi, I'm Jeff. We've met before, but I'm sorry, I can't remember your name." That's not as good as having it on hand, but better than faking it until you're mortified later when someone asks for an introduction.

At a business social, it's OK for your next question to be about the nature of his business. At other times, it'll depend on the time and place. In Washington, what you do is often more important than who you are, so it's perfectly courteous to segue from name to occupation. In other parts of the country, that kind of commercialism can blow a conversation clear out of the water.

Instead, lead with something appropriate. Canned conversations can work if you've got nothing else: "Say, how about the Steelers/weather/city council?" But it's better to use something situational: "I can't believe we keep coming back here, the beer's awful." "How about those Steelers (who are currently being shown on the TV)?" "How did you find out about this meeting?"

Small talk is just small talk—don't think you've made a connection on banalities alone. It's more graceful to let the conversation guide you to business topics, but it's usually all right to just switch tracks after a pause. I always pepper my speech with business asides to see if anyone picks up and switches tracks for me. "Oh, my Walkman radio? Yeah—it's very useful. National Public Radio has been doing a lot recently on the Internet—which is my business—so it's a good way to pass the time as I'm walking around."

It's always better to start by listening rather than telling. "What do you do?" slides in better than "I sell girdle grommets."

And, please, whatever you do—don't start small talk by commenting on the attributes of the hot blonde (male or female) at the end of the bar, unless you're in a strip joint, Hooters, or one of those other bastions of decency. If it's your style, you can agree strenuously when someone else brings it up, but there's an excellent chance that someone eavesdropping will be too pissed off at you to ever give you the chance to know them. Build a layer of trust before you fire into anything that might kill the conversation.

Body Language

Your body says more about you than you know. No matter what you're doing, the rest of your body is sending off signals letting the world know what is really going on inside. Most people pick these up only unconsciously, but that may be enough to scotch a contact early on.

When you're talking to someone, do you frequently look out the window for something that isn't there? Do you fidget with your fork? Do you absolutely need a drink or cigarette in your hand for your mouth to work? You're nervous, and more interested in making a good impression than in getting to know someone. Relax, and cut out the caffeine if you have to.

On the other end of the scale, are you making eye contact so ferociously that the other person starts stammering and looking away? Eye contact is a great way of being friendly—it's hardwired into our genetics after millions of years of being pack animals. But it's also the way we used to express herd dominance—and anyone you're trying to dominate is not going to be open to listening to you.

Make eye contact when you're speaking and listening, but break away appropriately to glance at—not watch—your food, your drink, the window, the TV. Then shift back to your partner before he starts thinking you're not listening.

Keep a distance between the two of you, especially if you're physically much bigger. Do not under any circumstances touch the other person—there are too many ways this gesture can be misread. Some people use flirtation as a means to generate business contacts, but in my mind you shouldn't turn on that charm unless you have a legitimate more-than-business interest. Mixing romantic and business signals is a great way to end up with a prospect who wants you to jump in the sack before you get their business.

Above all, be yourself. If you don't think you mix well in groups, think of social settings you *do* feel comfortable in, and imagine yourself there. You don't have to be a slave to your personality programming—just activate the friendliness, warmth, and outgoing nature that comes out when you're at ease. Before long, this personality switch will be automatic, and you won't have to think about bringing out your positive side in new situations.

Chutzpah in Business Theater

The making of a business contact involves a strict ritual—a ritual that can be avoided only at your peril. You can run through the various phases quickly or slowly, but you absolutely cannot skip them. They start with the initial contact, proceed with business-oriented conversation, and end with plans for follow-through.

The trading of business cards is part of the follow-through. There's a subclass of the business mingler who feels that the business card is part of the introduction—the idea being, I suppose, that if something better comes along and he has to break off conversation early, at least the prospect can get in touch with him later. The result of this is that you, the prospect, get home later, look at his card, and wonder, "Who the hell is this guy?" People don't need to know how to reach you until you convince them why they would want to.

The business conversation is a low-key method of trading information about your work and the clients you service. At this point, you should not be looking for a sale unless your prospect says something to the effect of, "I was thinking about getting something like that." With an opening like this, launch into a pitch—otherwise, just lay the groundwork for future conversations. Pushing for a sale before its time will leave your prospect with the same taste in his mouth as if he had just had a beer that had only fermented for two weeks.

Give more information to the prospect, but also get more from him. As wonderful as your product may be, not everyone will need it. And not everyone who needs it is a worthwhile use of your time. This is called "qualifying" the prospect as a worthwhile target. If you sell your services for a few thousand dollars a pop, and your prospect lets it be known that he's in the market for a $100 service, then he's probably not worth your time. But make sure he knows why he should call you when he can afford you.

And if you do discover that this person isn't worth your time, for God's sake don't show it. Gracefully extricate yourself at a good stopping point, and leave as if you have no choice in the matter: "Whoops, I see a client over there I need to speak to. Would you excuse me?" If nothing else, bring the conversation to a close, get up for another beer, and get distracted by someone else on the way back. Nothing is so rude as letting someone know in no uncertain terms that you're done with him, and cutting him off in mid-conversation does exactly that.

Finally, close with the follow-through. Business cards here are a must. Give him two or three if he's mentioned that he knows other people who might be interested in you. Always indicate that there will be something next. For un-qualified prospects, a simple "I guess I'll see you here next week, OK?" is fine. For more interesting prospects, say, "So I'll call you to discuss this further. How's Tuesday at 10 A.M.?" Or "I'll be sending you some materials; if I don't hear from you afterwards, I'll give you a call." The best prospects should be seen again in person. Ask them if they're free immediately following the meeting or schedule an appointment right there.

Chutzpah on the Telephone

The telephone is a great way to schmooze business. (Schmooze is another Yiddish term—it's a combination of socializing with ability and character, and frequently with a

C hutzpah has no textbook, but you can certainly bone up on your networking skills. Check out Susan RoAne's *How to Work a Room*. Not only does she give some great tips on getting wallflowers to blossom, but she likes chutzpah as much as I do.

deeper agenda.) No travel time required, and you can knock the contact off your to-do list much faster than you usually can in person.

When you call, say first who you're calling for, then give your name and company name. Don't fret if you're a company of one; the receptionist doesn't know that. If you're asked for the reason for the call, don't lie and say you're returning a call if you're not. Give a concise description of the purpose of the call. (Which means you should have one ready.)

If you get your target on the line, give a quick description of why you're calling. It's all right to go straight to a short pitch, but precede it with something personalized so they know you have a reason for calling them specifically. Say something like, "I just received your mailing about your product, and I thought you'd be interested in knowing how my services can help make it better," but in much more specific terms. If your target is uninterested, try to get him to agree to read your materials, and then let him go. Don't try to keep him on the line; seconds count on the telephone, and a minute over your allotted time will make a very bad impression.

When you can't get through, leave a message with a specific set of times you'll be waiting for a call back. Ask the prospect to tell you a good time to call if he gets your machine. And if, after a few rounds of telephone tag, it seems clear that your prospect isn't interested in speaking with you, ask a receptionist for a fax number and send a one-page letter detailing why you've called.

Most people will make time for you if you give them reason to. A professional demeanor and respect for the other person's time are often reason enough.

Making Your Luck and Making Your Fortune

The Western world has a very skewed idea of what constitutes luck. Most of us believe that some people are just lucky, other people are just unlucky, and that's all there is to it.

Hogwash. The guy who hit the lottery for $1,000 yesterday appears to be lucky, until you hear that he spent $2,000 on tickets in the last year. The guy who shut down his business last year seems unlucky, except that he met his wife through his first venture and now the two of them are going into a new business together.

There are two kinds of luck: normal and paranormal. Everyone gets normal luck fairly frequently; it's dictated by the law of probability. If your train arrives every eight minutes and takes a minute to leave the platform, then once in every eight times you take the train, you'll get lucky and the train will be there when you arrive, no waiting.

Normal luck is what makes hardworking businesspeople lucky. When you meet a group of prospects, a certain percentage of those prospects will be qualified targets, and a certain percentage of those qualified prospects will become sales. Lucky entrepreneurs are just like the guy who bought 2,000 lottery tickets: shoot enough times, and you'll make more hits than the guy who tries less often.

Hard work can also change the percentages. A change in marketing can increase the odds of landing a qualified prospect from 10 percent to 20 percent. In other words, hard work can increase your normal luck both by giving you more chances and by increasing the odds that any one of them will pay off.

There's another kind of luck, which I call paranormal luck. It's the gift from God that falls on you when you least expect it, seemingly beyond any control that you had.

I had paranormal luck once my first year. I came back from a trip in which I had overextended my finances, and I was flat broke with bills past due. The next day I got a brand new Visa card in the mail, along with three credit rejection letters since my credit was shot to hell. That card floated me until my next check came in.

It was paranormal luck—I had applied for the card with no expectation of getting it—but still, I had applied for that card. Hard work opens the door to paranormal luck as well as regular luck. If luck hits you often enough, you'll be hard-pressed to tell the difference between the two.

I am firmly convinced that there are charmed people in this world. I am equally convinced that I am one of them. There have been at least two moments in my life where, but for amazing paranormal luck, I would no longer be breathing. That does a lot to convince one of the charm.

Charms are a combination of supernatural forces and personality. It doesn't matter if you have a guardian angel sitting on your shoulder if you don't give her the opportunity to make things right for you. People who expect bad things out of their lives get them because they aren't looking for the good. Conversely, people who expect the best frequently get it—because their temperaments make the bad quickly forgotten.

And there are times when mere mortals can wield almost supernatural powers in the quest for success. Call it God helping those who help themselves, or call it magic. I have seen it, and it works. If you believe you can work magic, before long you will.

CHAPTER 11

A Walk Through a Successful Sale

*Y*ou've got all the ingredients for whipping up sales right now, but just to be certain you've got the process down pat, we're going to do a run–through.

It will be very important to your business and to your personal equilibrium that you develop a procedure for keeping track of where all your prospects and clients are on the sales time line at all times. You'll be doing several follow-ups for each client, so this will help ensure that no one falls through the cracks.

Step One: The Contact

First will be the moment when the prospect falls into your lap. It might be when you meet him somewhere, or when he responds to your marketing. Even though it's early in the relationship, the contact can occur at any point along the sales time line. Some prospects will have their checkbooks ready, others will want more information, and still others will have no interest in your product and only be wasting your time.

The contact is where you start qualifying the prospect, determining if his needs and your service are a good fit. Don't try to slam him into a sale if your product will be a procrustean bed for his needs, and you'll have to chop off his legs to get him to fit. That's a good way to generate a long list of unhappy customers.

Step Two: The Pitch

Lay out the advantages of your products as thoroughly and concisely as you can. It's not necessary to give every last detail—you don't need to mention that it can cause cancer in laboratory rats when used as a skin ointment, but you should say quickly that it's not good for smokers. Be ready with details when prospects ask for them.

Stay attuned at all times to how well you're doing with the prospect. When he's ready to give you the sale, shut up and skip to the close. I've seen people talk their way out of sales because they didn't know when to stop yammering on. They accidentally hit that one small detail that's actually a negative in the eyes of the prospect, and the sale is lost. (Of course, that detail will come up later, but once the sale commitment is made, it'll be easier to work around it to accommodate the customer.)

Of course, you'll also want to determine if he can afford you. This will be harder to tell, but a good sign is the length of time that passes between the time you quote your price and your prospect's next words. A pause of a few seconds or even an intake of breath is a good clue that you're not talking to a new customer.

And don't make the mistake I used to make, filling up that pause with qualifiers that might lower your price. Many people use silence as a negotiation tool; if there's dead time for fifteen seconds after you quote a price, keep your mouth shut and let the time pass. If you begin wondering if your prospect has died, say, "Are you there?" but never, "We can reduce that price."

Step Three: The Close

When the prospect has asked all the questions she can think of, or when she seems amenable to reaching for her wallet, close the sale. That means ask for it. Many failed salesmen give great pitches but have trouble asking for money.

There are books filled with techniques on the art of closing, and it can be very difficult with some clients. No matter how much they love the service, they haven't agreed to buy it until you've made the close, and a poorly handled close can ruin the sale.

If you can, ask for the sale in a way that avoids a yes or no answer. When things are going well, I say, "So what time should we schedule a consulting session?" rather than "Should we schedule?" If things are still iffy, I'll close with a "should," but follow that up with "I'm free on Tuesday and Thursday of next week." The chance for a "no" is still there, but the more real I make the sale seem, the more likely it is to occur.

Most people instinctively want to wait until later to close the sale. They'll tell you to call them back, or they'll call you, and buy your product then. That usually means no. By the time you reach them, you might have to re-pitch, and it won't be as persuasive the second time. Better to get the sale now by conveying a sense of urgency.

Since I'm a consultant, I can't very well say that the product will go bad if it's not purchased immediately, so I put a time pressure on with a a special pricing offer: any clients who pay me up front for services they receive later get a 10 percent bonus on their payments against my future work. Pay me $1,000 and get $1,100 worth of work. This is slightly cheaper for me than a 10 percent discount—do the math and you'll see that a 10 percent bonus is only a 9.09 percent discount. And I can't very well put a deadline on a discount, warning my clients that if they don't hire me now, I'll charge them more later. But giving them an incentive to pay me up-front cash has done wonders for my bottom line. It's easily the best billing idea I've ever had, and I don't know anyone else who does it. Incidentally, it started as a 20 percent bonus, but I've wised up since then.

Do what it takes to close the sale—bonuses, discounts, additional services. Then get that check up front if you can.

The last step of the close is getting it in writing. Every last point should be spelled out and agreed upon by both of you. I've skipped this step in favor of a handshake deal a number of times, and I've been burned by it.

Step Four: The Service

It goes without saying that your service or product must be exemplary. It doesn't matter if you're the nicest guy on

Earth, give a shoddy product and your client won't feel he's getting his money's worth. Everything you do in the course of providing a service has one and only one goal: making the client happy. Thrilled, even.

The less you promise in the pitch and the close, the easier it will be to overwhelm his expectations. If at all possible, hold back a little when telling the client about some of the features you normally provide, and then surprise the hell out of him when you give him more than he asked for.

Step Five: The Invoice

Don't ask me why, but many people feel uncomfortable asking for the money that's due them. If you've provided a service and the client owes you some bucks, send him a bill. If he doesn't pay you, call him. Then send another one. And keep it up.

On a long-term project, agree up front that you'll bill him regularly and expect payment throughout. Biweekly is good for work that's done every week; switch to monthly for more sporadic work. If you bill too infrequently, the client may be surprised by costs that seem too high; more frequent, smaller bills are more palatable.

Set up a penalty for late payments. I charge 2 percent for every thirty days a bill is overdue, and my invoice clearly states that my fees are due upon receipt of the bill. I've never had to charge a late fee, but as I write this, a single client owes me $37.50. He'll be getting a bill this week for $38.25. Next month, it'll be up to $39.02. I personally don't care about the extra 75¢, but I'm hoping the increase will spur him to pay the rest of the money. Since each month I'll be compound 2 percent interest on the previous month's interest, I'll essentially be billing him a pretty high 27 percent a year. With larger bills, late fees can be quite significant—but then you'll be waiting on a really massive check. No matter how you slice it, if you get into a late billing situation, both of you lose.

When I finally get the client to pay, I'll waive the interest if he asks me to and I haven't been waiting too long. It's a convenient bargaining chip. But if a client pulls this more than once, he'll be paying me up front from now on, with no bonus.

If a client is stupid enough to pull this on you while you're still providing the service, cut him off. (Some clients will try to negotiate contractually that you can't do this; avoid this clause at all costs.) You're providing your time and effort in return for cash, not goodwill.

Step Six: The Follow-Through

After the service is done, ask the client what he thought of it. Suggest new jobs you can do for him or additional products you sell, based on what you've learned about his business from the first project. Repeat business is the best kind of business since it's so much easier than finding new clients— but if you don't ask for it, you probably won't get it.

Past clients should be treated as your best prospects; send them all your mailings and frequently drop them personalized messages suggesting new ideas you've had, or even other resources (aside from your business) that might interest them. The more you do for them, the more they'll do for you.

Step Seven: The Overview

Every six months or so, go back over all your client records. Pick out a few lucrative contracts that you'd like to restart, and put them high on your prospect list. Schedule meetings or send them gifts, just do something that puts you back on their payroll.

An excellent way to do this is to create a questionnaire quizzing clients about your services. You'll get valuable feedback about your quality and shortcomings, and you can write it so that it acts as a marketing piece: "Are you aware that we are offering a discount of 25 percent on sales of 10,000 widgets?" "Would you be interested in service X, which we are considering introducing?"

From the first time you meet the client until, well, death, you should be building and nurturing the relationship. A sale is only the first step in that process. Don't drop the ball after the check is in hand.

When Things Go Wrong

Someday you're going to have an unhappy customer. I had one once when I didn't have a written contract. I thought I was going to provide about ten hours of services for a flat rate. She thought I was going to do everything on a whole laundry list of ideas that I had written to her three months prior to our agreement.

Things got ugly at our last meeting. I assumed that my work was done. She was thinking, "Wait, that's it?" And she asked me when I was going to start those other services.

This one took me by surprise, and I rather testily replied that to do all that work, I'd be billing myself out at 10¢ an hour, and frankly I thought I was worth more. The meeting ended frostily, but I recovered by talking to her privately afterward. I asked, "It's obvious that you don't feel you've gotten your money's worth. What other work would make you satisfied that you had?" By phrasing it that way, I kept her away from that laundry list, and negotiated the minimum amount of extra services that would make her happy.

I did those jobs quickly, and then I took my check and headed for the hills. She was satisfied enough that I knew I might still get referrals from her in the future, but I never prospected her again. The miscommunication was entirely my fault—but any client who has such unrealistic expectations about my time is going to be serious trouble in the future.

Keep 'em happy, then decide if you want to keep them at all.

CHAPTER 12

Expansion Without Stretch Marks

*T*here comes a point in many ventures when the owner must decide whether to expand the business with new employees. This may come on Day One, if the business absolutely requires additional help to get off the ground. Or it may come years later.

Adding employees is an awesome responsibility. You will owe them far more than they owe you. They will only be giving you labor, but you will be giving them their livelihoods. If you have to postpone a payday during a down period, their personal lives may become tumultuous; close the business and you may ruin their financial lives along with your own.

On top of that, even in the best of circumstances employees add major costs and headaches in terms of benefits, government regulations, and accountants' fees. For all of these reasons, we'll start our discussion of expansion by first exploring ways to *not* hire new people.

Cutting the Deadwood

In this era of downsizing, deadwood frequently refers to unproductive staff. More valuable may be cutting out unprofitable clients.

Most entrepreneurs instinctively try to become all things to all people, especially in the early days when they desperately need business. If you've done this, you're probably following the 80/20 rule: 80 percent of your business is coming from 20 percent of your clients. Eighty percent of your headaches are coming from a different 20 percent.

Trimming back customers is anathema to most business owners—but when so much of your time is being sucked up by a small number of clients, is it really worth it to keep them on? How much more could you be making—without adding new people—if you devoted your time to those 20 percent who make up the bulk of your income?

Businesses naturally outgrow their original clients as they take new directions and follow different goals. Don't carry along old clients for the ride. Cut them off as professionally as possible, perhaps by referring them to your competition, and go on to better things.

Adding Brainpower

If the support you need is more in the visionary department than in the day-to-day tasks, get yourself a support group that you don't have to pay.

A board of advisors is the sole proprietor's equivalent of the corporation's board of directors. Ideally, it's made up of a small number of people you respect who have a broad range of experience that can be brought to bear on your company. You gather them together, tell them everything about your business (warts and all), and get their feedback on where the business should go.

Advisors can be compensated very modestly—in many cases just buying them lunch may be enough to keep them coming back every three months. But why not put your money where their mouths are: give them a stake in the business by paying them some small percentage of your net profits. That will increase their interest in seeing you succeed, and maybe even get some of them to help implement the plans you'll be generating.

If the day-to-day work of your business has left you too tired for long-range planning, don't hire someone to free you for the brain work. Get a board of advisors to help you plan the future, and use the energy you save to make the day-to-day operations better than ever.

Hire Contracts, Not Bodies

Contracted employees can make expansion much easier. They're paid in cash, receive no benefits, and have almost no requirements imposed on them by the federal government. You don't have to worry about work rules, benefits, or whether to hire salaried or hourly employees. You just tell them what to do, and they hop to it.

The problem is that the IRS is wise to employers who try to get around their rules by calling their employees contractors. There's a twenty-step test to see if a worker is a contractor or an employee.

It's to your benefit to hire workers who are independent contractors, as opposed to actual employees. You don't have to withhold or pay taxes on payments to contractors. With employees, on the other hand, you must withhold income taxes, withhold and pay Social Security and Medicare taxes, and pay unemployment taxes.

To help you determine whether you can classify a worker as a contractor, the IRS has issued twenty guidelines.

Not every guideline is applicable to every situation, and the degree of importance of each factor varies depending on the type of work and individual circumstances. However, all relevant factors should be considered in making a determination, and no one factor is decisive.

It does not matter if a written agreement exists stating that the work relationship is one way if the facts indicate otherwise. If an employer treats an employee as an independent contractor, the person responsible for the collection and payment of withholding taxes may be held personally liable for an amount equal to the taxes that should have been withheld.

Employee or Contractor?

The following are the twenty guidelines, excerpted from IRS Publication 937, 1995 edition:

1. **Instructions.** An employee must comply with instructions about when, where, and how to work. Even if no instructions are given, the employer still has the right to control how work results are achieved.
2. **Training.** An employee may be trained to perform services in a particular manner. Independent contractors ordinarily use their own methods and receive no training from the purchasers of their services.
3. **Integration.** An employee's services are usually integrated into the business operations because the services are important to the success or continuation of the business. This shows that the employee is subject to direction and control.

(continues)

4. **Services Rendered Personally.** An employee renders services personally. This shows that the employer is interested in the methods as well as the results.

5. **Hiring Assistants.** An employee works for an employer who hires, supervises, and pays workers. An independent contractor can hire, supervise, and pay assistants under a contract that requires him or her to provide materials and labor and to be responsible only for the result.

6. **Continuing Relationship.** An employee generally has a continuing relationship with an employer. A continuing relationship may exist even if work is performed at recurring although irregular intervals.

7. **Set Hours of Work.** An employee usually has set number of hours of work established by an employer. An independent contractor generally can set his or her own work hours.

8. **Full-Time Required.** An employee may be required to work or to be available full-time. This indicates control by the employer. An independent contractor can work when and for whom he or she chooses.

9. **Work Done on the Premises.** An employee usually works on the premises of an employer's business, or works on a route or at a location designated by an employer.

10. **Sequence of Work Set.** An employee may be required to perform services in the order set by an employer. This shows that the employee is subject to direction and control.

11. **Reports.** An employee may be required to submit reports to an employer. This shows that the employer maintains a degree of control.

12. **Payments.** An employee is generally paid by the hour, week, or month. An independent contractor is usually paid by the job or on a straight commission.

13. **Expenses.** An employee's business and travel expenses are generally paid by an employer. This shows that the employee is subject to regulation and control.

14. **Tools and Materials.** An employee is normally furnished significant tools, materials, and other equipment by an employer.

15. **Investment.** An independent contractor has a significant investment in the facilities he or she uses in performing services for someone else.

16. **Profit or Loss.** An independent contractor can make a profit or suffer a loss.

17. **Works for More than One Person or Firm.** An independent contractor is generally free to provide his or her services to two or more unrelated persons or firms at the same time.

18. **Offers Services to the Public.** An independent contractor makes his or her services available to the public.
19. **Right to Fire.** An employee can be fired by an employer. An independent contractor cannot be fired so long as he or she produces a result that meets the specifications of the contract.
20. **Right to Quit.** An employee can quit his or her job at any time without incurring liability. An independent contractor usually agrees to complete a specific job and is responsible for its satisfactory completion, or is legally obligated to make good for failure to complete it.

As you can see, the rules basically say that you can have workers on contract provided you give them plenty of leeway in how they do their work for you. But isn't that the '90s goal of the empowered employee? Find yourself people who can take responsibility for setting their own working hours and environment, parcel out a project to them, and turn them loose. The better you have communicated your needs to them, the more likely they'll be to surprise you with more than you ask— for the same reasons you do this for your clients.

Some ideas for hiring contractors:

- Give them small jobs first. See if they're up to your standards. If not, let them go after the first contract.
- Set up strict reporting requirements so you know exactly what stage each project is in.
- Tell your contractors, and write into their contracts, that payment will be made only when a job is completed to your satisfaction. If the work is shoddy, pay them a percentage of what adequate work would have earned and let them go—then find someone who can do it better. On the other hand, fast, quality work should receive a bonus. Don't contract the bonus, just pay it when you're pleasantly surprised—and you can turn that quality into more income from your clients.

- If your contractors are interacting with your clients, give them guidelines on what they can and cannot do in representing your company. Give them titles they can use, a budget they can spend in completing each project, and limits on the authority they can assume. And check with an attorney to make sure that these rules don't put you into the employee doghouse with the IRS.
- Speaking of the IRS, you've got to file a 1099 form for every contractor to whom you pay more than $600 a year (at the time of this writing; check with the IRS for changes to the minimum).

A s might be guessed, the IRS *loves* classifying people as employees. That means more taxes are collected, and with much less work on their part, since tracking down contractors requires collating tons of 1099 forms instead of just one W-2 employee form. This has caused no small amount of consternation on the part of many small-business owners, since the twenty rules for contractors are written so poorly. Just about anyone can be seen as an employee based on a narrow interpretation of the rules, including the kid you pay $10 to shovel your walk—if you give him your shovel and tell him to get it done by this afternoon.

As a result, many entrepreneurs play cat and mouse with the IRS. Hire a bunch of people, call them contractors, and then hope that Uncle Sam doesn't call you in for an audit. If the IRS decides that you're an employer, you can get socked with mucho back taxes and penalties. So document all of the ways in which you follow their rules, and if you're in doubt, check with an attorney.

No Choice, Gotta Have 'Em

If you absolutely must have full-time or part-time employees, which will be true for most retail businesses, then just bite the bullet and go with it. Your first stop should be a visit with a good business lawyer. Get a list of requirements and steps to take in setting up your business to legally hire employees for your state and community. Expect to start paying money to accountants or a benefits firm, too, after you've made your first hire.

A good place to get an idea of what you're in for is the Internal Revenue Service's Publication 937, *Employment Taxes*. It lays out all the rules that define who is an employee and who isn't, and then tells you what you have to do to legally employ someone.

Hiring employees is potentially the biggest pitfall of the small business, which is why I've avoided it entirely. There's far more to it than we can cover here. Hit any entrepreneurial bookshelf, and you'll find whole books devoted to the hiring process, motivating employees, covering yourself legally, and letting people go. The following are some tips to get you started, but I strongly recommend doing additional research and consulting an attorney before you take this plunge.

- *Hire People Who Complement Your Abilities.* It's common for entrepreneurs to find people who are similar to themselves; these are the people with whom you most quickly build rapport. But avoid doubling up on people who can do well what you can do well. It's far better to find people whose strengths are your weaknesses.

- *That's* Complement, *not* Compliment. Find employees who aren't afraid to speak their minds and disagree with you when they find it necessary. The entrepreneur is an ego-driven beast; hire someone whose sole purpose is to feed your ego, and he won't feed your wallet.

- *Hire Only the Best.* Don't settle for second best or take the first person who comes along in a crisis. The first person you hire who is slightly lower than your standards will introduce a new bottom level of competence for your other employees, who may relax their own standards accordingly.

- *Develop an Interview Process, and Check It with an Attorney.* There are a whole range of questions that you can't ask during the interview, including health issues and the prospective employee's plans to have children. At the same time, you'll want to make sure that your interviews give you all the information you need to make the right choice.

- *Keep an Eye on Them.* Employees can do all sorts of horrible things to their bosses, including walking off with the day's receipts or half the inventory. Make sure you have ways of corroborating what they tell you about sales and income, and be very discriminating about who gets the right to write checks and dole out cash.

- *Treat Them Well.* Pay them what they are worth, either with good salaries or with bonuses indexed to profits. (That's *profits,* not sales; keep tabs on how much money they make for you, not on how much product they move.) Establish benefits plans as early as possible. Look for cost-free benefits, such as flexible work schedules and employee-led cross-training sessions. Make your business an enjoyable place to work, and your employees will reward you.

- *Be Your Own Best Employee.* If you insist employees show up at eight A.M., don't saunter in at 9:30. Your employees will look to you to set the work standards, no matter how dedicated or talented they are.

- *Learn from Them.* Treat your employees like human beings; listen to what they have to say, even if it's in an area that's firmly your bailiwick. I'm partial to the Captain Picard style of management. Whenever he said, "Make it so," he brooked no argument, but at the same time he listened to and considered what even the greenest ensign had to say.

CHAPTER 13

Staying on Top

*A*n entrepreneur has a lot to do and even more to keep track of. I've been constantly revising my organizational systems. It's an uphill battle as my business expands and more people have legitimate claims on my time and energy. If I did not evaluate my tools on an ongoing basis, and chuck old systems that were hindering me, I'd have been swamped long ago (or, I should say, even *more* swamped, since it still gets pretty hectic).

A number of new and old technologies can help. Here are some of the best ways I've found to maintain my equilibrium *and* my sanity.

This Isn't the Telephone Ma Bell Used!

The telephone is the most powerful tool you have to communicate with clients quickly and efficiently. Unlike e-mail and faxes, just about everyone has a telephone and is comfortable using it to do business. I still prefer face-to-face meetings when time permits, but you can't beat a telephone conference for eliminating travel time, dressing time (from my casual look to something that won't scare children in public), and the distractions that always seem to happen when I'm out and about.

And telephones can do a hell of a lot more than they used to. New computerized services offered by most phone companies can go a long way toward keeping your communications and your life organized.

Voice-mail systems act as computerized answering machines, taking calls when you're not there. They have several advantages over machines, though, most notably the ability to quickly zap through any number of messages to get to the one you want. They can also delete some messages and leave others for later. I use my voice-mail box as a to-do list, deleting the calls I've returned and leaving others for later.

Another advantage of my voice-mail system, which I get directly from my phone company, is that it picks up calls when the line is busy. I find this far preferable, and far more professional, than Call Waiting. Call Waiting is the popular home service that allows you to hear when a second call is coming through, so you can switch back and forth between two conversations. This inevitably sends a message to the person you're speaking to that anyone who calls next is more important than she is. I got into the habit of checking my voice mail after every call, so I can continue my calls uninterrupted.

IdentaRing is a feature that allows you to have multiple phone numbers without the expense of multiple lines. You add a second phone number to your first line; when people call you on that second number, it rings the phone differently than with the main number. I use the same line for personal and business calls, and I use the ringing sound to let me know whether to say, "Hello?" or "Millennium Consulting, can I help you?" Each IdentaRing number has its own voice-mail box, so my incoming calls are divided into personal and business messages.

During crunch times, there may be some calls you'll want to take but others you'd rather put off until later. Caller ID is a method of screening incoming calls before you answer the phone. A small screen lights up as the phone rings, indicating the phone number and sometimes the name of the person calling. You can then decide whether to take the call. Caller ID boxes also remember the last several incoming calls, so you can quickly scan to see which messages to take.

Road Warrior Telephone Tactics

If your business requires you to be frequently out of the office, you'll want a phone service you can take with you.

The obvious answer is a cellular phone. Cell-phone service is expensive, although new competition is gradually driving the price down. Cell phones typically cost $30 to $40 for a certain number of minutes each month; time after that is billed at 10¢ to 40¢ a minute. Expect to pay as much as $2 more a minute if you're calling or receiving a call outside your "home area," which is usually your state. The phones themselves are frequently free if you sign up for a fixed contract of a year or two. Cell phones are an expensive but very useful time-saver. Mine allows me to make several calls and catch up on my messages while I'm on foot between meetings.

Pagers are another way to keep in touch with your clients. Just give your pager number to those you wish to have access to you, and when they call, a message will appear on your pager unit telling you who called and perhaps a brief message. I considered a pager before I bought a cellular phone, but decided against it. A cell phone lets me call people wherever I am, and gives me the option to take incoming calls or let my voice mail handle them. A pager gives your clients twenty-four-hour access to you. That's a bit more available than I want to be, so count me among the beeperless.

The single most useful service I have is my AT&T EasyReach system. It's a 500 number—that is, it uses 500 as its area code. I can forward my 500-number calls to any telephone in the world; clients can call my 500 number to reach me without having any idea where I am. (If it's an international call, they're warned before the call goes through, since they're paying for it.) I can even program the number to try me at any of three different phone numbers before it hits my voice-mail system.

You can call your phone company for more information about any of the above services; you can get information about EasyReach by calling AT&T at (800) 222-0300.

Information Organizers

While you're on the go, you'll want to have a lot of information at your fingertips. Executive types can just call their secretaries to get addresses, phone numbers, and schedules. Entrepreneurs have to rely on their own devices.

The simplest way to keep information is with a pen and paper. If you're hyper-organized, you can probably get by with a small notebook divided into sections. Use the first section for phone numbers, the second for scheduling, the third as a to-do list, and later sections as a scratch pad for recording new information before you divide it into one of the other areas.

Many people swear by their personal organizers, which take the above idea one step further by providing preprinted pages for recording all sorts of information. You can get inserts for everything from lifetime goal planning to calorie counting. Some of the most popular systems include Franklin and Filofax; any well-stocked stationery store should have a number of brands to choose from. Expect to pay top dollar for the leather-bound organizers; cheaper models can frequently be found with a little shopping.

I despise using pen and paper for just about anything, so a godsend for me has been my minicassette recorder. Anything that I would normally write down I record into the sixty-minute tape. Once a day I transcribe the tape and get all of the information into my computer, where I keep my schedule, to-do lists, and list of contacts. The cassette recorder fits into a suit-jacket pocket, and I always keep it handy, so whenever a thought strikes me I can get it onto the tape and forget about it.

The next tech level up is a personal digital assistant, a small calculator-sized device that holds schedules, to-do lists, and contact information. These start at around $20 for small models that can hold a few hundred names and go up to $700 for the fancy Apple Newton, which can fax messages; "beam" information invisibly to other nearby Newtons, computers, and printers; and connect you to Internet and pager services. I used to run my life based upon one of these, and I might do so again someday soon. It can be a lifesaver to have your entire Rolodex on call at any time.

Finally, I use a calendar and organization program on my computer as the main way of keeping my life in order. There are dozens software programs available. I use the excellent Now Contact and Now Up-to-Date ($99 for the pair), which are only available for the Macintosh. (I've heard great things about Lotus Organizer, which sells for $129 and is available for IBM-compatible computers only.) These programs, usually called PIMs or personal information managers, give you far more flexibility than any digital assistant or pen-and-paper system can. Once your information is stored in the program, you can spit out weekly and monthly schedules, phone lists, and just about any other format you can think of. I divide my contacts into personal and various business categories; when business is slow, I call up a list of clients in a particular category and start making phone calls. And when I'm traveling, I can look up all of my friends in the city I'm in. Once you get used to working with information this way, you won't know how you lived without it.

Controlling Your Time

Multiple overlapping deadlines are the scourge of every entrepreneur. I wish I could tell you that my life runs like a well-oiled machine, but too often it's more like one of those 1890s flying machines crashing into a barn.

Rule one is to keep a constant list of things that have to get done. Note that I said "a list" and not "lists." Multiple lists are a quick way to insanity and inefficiency. Keep everything in one place where you can get an overview of your life at a quick glance.

The system I'm using now consists of two sections: ongoing projects and quick to-dos. I sort the ongoing projects by the imminence of their deadlines and enter the to-dos in my calendar on the days they need to get done. If a bill needs to go out on Friday, I'll put it on my Wednesday to-do list. The first priority on any given day is to knock off as many to-dos as possible; then I devote the rest of my time to ongoing projects. To-dos that don't get completed are moved to the following day, with a note that indicates whether the next day is the absolute deadline for completion. I use my PIM to take care of this, but you can do the same thing with a simple pad of paper. Just use the first section for your ongoing project list and reserve a sheet of paper a day to list your upcoming to-dos.

Your greatest enemy will be overcommitment. The simplest way to make sure you get everything done is not to commit to more than you can do in a reasonable workweek. My schedule is always crazy because I am still learning how to accurately judge my time. Keep track of how long a particular to-do or project takes, and then don't schedule more of them than you can handle. If this means turning down business to maintain a reasonable quality of life, that's an adequate trade-off.

Stemming the Paper Tide

In my opinion, the best way to handle paperwork is with a flamethrower. Barring that, it's guaranteed that you'll be drowning in paper unless you come up with a system for handling it. My rule of thumb: touch paper only once, the first time you read it, and then deal with it immediately or file it.

I use stackable shelves to keep track of all my paper. Everything that comes in over the course of a day goes into a box labeled "Newly In." I toss it in there immediately and forget about it until I can get to it later the same day.

Below that box is "To File." Anything that should be saved for posterity gets left in there until it starts to overflow, at which point I put it into my long-term filing system.

Beneath that is "To Mail." Outgoing letters go there until I can envelope them, stamp them, and get them on their merry way.

On the bottom, "Urgent." This is my in-box equivalent of the to-do list. If a piece of paper needs immediate attention, it goes into this box. It then gets handled along with all of my to-do items for the day.

Anything else that comes in that will be a future to-do item, such as next week's bills, goes into an expandable folder I purchased for this use. It's got thirty-one sections numbered, appropriately, one through thirty-one. A letter that needs a reply on the fifteenth of next month goes into the "15" section. Each morning I move today's batch from the folder to the Urgent box. On those rare occasions when a letter needs to be dealt with more than a month later, I'll file it with a note as to which month it needs handling—but most items that are that non-urgent can be safely skipped entirely.

The monthly folder is also useful for recurring expense reminders. I have a note in there to pay off my MasterCard

---

T he best time-management book available is Stephen Covey's _First Things First_. For the long haul, when you're deciding what to do with your life and how to manage your affairs to reach your goals, check out his ideas in _The Seven Habits of Highly Effective People_.

every month, the note comes out, I write the check, and then it goes back into the same folder for next month.

Once a week or so, I transfer everything in my "To File" box into my long-term files. I use a hierarchical system of folders: a section for Millennium work, a section for my writing, a section for the Noodle Club, etc. Each section is subdivided as much as necessary so that I can find whatever I'm looking for quickly. I have many folders with only one sheet of paper in them—manila folders are cheap, and my time isn't.

I personally don't see the point of long-term storage if the stuff that's stored is never looked at again. Every six months I go through my files and see what's there. Usually about 10 percent of it is for projects that never took off, clients who have died or been captured by alien invaders, and other useless paper. I cull that out and trash it. Then again, I'm always careful to save old ideas, which occasionally I decide to revive. Those gems make it back into my Urgent file and daily to-do lists.

Anal-Compulsive Record Keeping

The IRS requires you to keep track of expense-related paperwork, receipts, and income. If push ever comes to shove and you're invited to have lunch with one of their friendly agents while they go over your tax filings, the more accurately you can document each and every item you have, the healthier you'll be.

But so long as you're forced to be anal for the IRS, why not also be anal for yourself? Every once in a while a client will ask you a question expecting you to remember what you told them eighteen months ago, or you'll need to refer to an old phone conversation to explain why the client still owes you money, or why you don't owe the client any more time or product.

During these moments, it's useful to say, "My notes indicate that you said that during our conversation at 11 A.M. last February fifteenth." That at least shows that you know what *you're* talking about—it's up to the client to prove you wrong. (Still, it's usually best to lose gracefully to keep the client happy.)

Get in the habit of anally recording what you do, what you say, and who you say it to. Write up a brief paragraph of notes immediately after every meeting or phone call, and record it in your PIM or on paper in a folder with the client's name. An offhand comment today could be a whole new source of revenue in six months. Keeping track will help you stay on track.

CHAPTER 14

Keeping Unbalanced

*M*ost self-help books warn you to keep a certain balance to your life by finding your core values and beliefs and dividing your work and social time in a way that is harmonious with your goals.

To which I say, lots of luck. I wouldn't recognize a balanced life if I tripped over it. I was none too stable before I started a business, and since then it's been all downhill.

Finding balance on a roller-coaster is a pretty insane task. But that doesn't mean you can't find happiness. It's just a matter of recognizing your life for what it is and taking joy out of it wherever you can. There's nothing balanced about that at all. If anything, the entrepreneur's ability to deal with a constantly "overbalanced" life—in which the tottering pile of demands keeps you running from one commitment to another—gives you the edge necessary for survival and success.

So get used to imbalance—and learn to enjoy it.

The Goals You Will Never Meet

All entrepreneurs share certain personality traits. Even if you're not aware of them all, it's a given that you'll stumble across them eventually. Entrepreneuring nurtures these traits even if you're not born with them.

You're a perfectionist, in small ways if not in the big picture. No task will ever be completed to your satisfaction, even if it's good enough for the client.

You're going to raise the pole-vaulting bar every time you make a successful leap, whether you know it or not. What you treat as a major success today will not be good enough six months from now, and so on. The hunger for victory will continually devour each project you feed it, and then send you looking for more.

You're going to expect every risk you take to pay off, and quickly. When the reward shows up slowly or not at all, you won't remember that it was never guaranteed; instead, you'll blame yourself for its loss.

You're going to expect of yourself nothing less than papal infallibility and omnipotence. When you only hit 90 percent, you'll focus on the 10 percent you missed instead of the 90 percent you achieved.

Sounds like a grueling course, doesn't it? Where's the satisfaction, the joys, the pat on the back for a job well done?

That's up to you—you'll have to decide for yourself what's good enough. Your instinct will be to say that nothing is ever good enough, to focus on the few failures rather than on the many successes.

If there's been one thing I regret about my life's course so far, it's that I can understand this concept intellectually, but I haven't yet learned it emotionally. Follow in my footsteps here, and you'll be setting yourself up for far more misery and stress than you have to.

It's your life, and quite probably the only shot you'll have at it. If you're not enjoying yourself, what's the point? Slack off every once in a while, and give yourself some rewards and recognition. Do whatever it takes to recharge your batteries. Then jump back in the fray and try living up to your principles again, doing what it takes to conquer your demons.

Risk Without Insecurity

Risk is the natural environment of the entrepreneur. The greatest risk comes when you first start the business, but with hard work, experience, and luck, it will substantially reduce over time. Risk can be minimized, but it can never be eradicated entirely.

This is part of life as well as business, and it can truly be said that risk is a part of any career, entrepreneurial or not. But for entrepreneurs, risk is much more personal, since it's undertaken on the entrepreneur's authority alone, with no one else to share the brunt of the damage if it does not pay off.

Running a business is a constant exercise in stretching your talents and capabilities, as well as those of your staff, associates, and company as a whole. Like sharks and Woody Allen's love affairs, the business has to constantly move into new waters; there is very little opportunity to rest on one's laurels.

There is nothing new in this statement; many people have become rich in the last few years by coming up with new synonyms for the word "change" and new ways to charge executives thousands of dollars for the privilege of repeating the obvious. Less discussed are the psychological effects on the business owner when the business and his own professional and personal psyche must be reinvented on a regular—sometimes it seems daily—basis.

War veterans and survivors of violent experiences often develop a condition known as post-traumatic stress disorder as they try to cope with what they have seen. It is often simpler for the sufferer to cope with his experiences if he has been removed from the environment that caused the stress in the first place.

Coping with stress is much more difficult when the stressors cannot be removed. Risk naturally involves stress, and constant risk can bring with it constant stress. If you want to avoid living that kind of life, you must do two things: you must take control of the kinds of risks you are taking, and you must manage the effects these risks have on your temperament and outlook.

It's Supposed to Be Hard!

First off, keep reminding yourself that what you are doing is challenging. Most of us had years on end in school when we coasted along—or were tempted to—using skills and "good enough" standards that we knew would get us by without causing us to break a sweat. Running a business is not like that at all. Entrepreneurs who coast end up looking for jobs before too long. The work you do will be tough, and frequently you may find yourself nearly overwhelmed by the demands of the work and your own limited experience in dealing with them.

When you're in this position, congratulations! It's a good indication you're doing things right. And rest assured that you will get better at what you're doing. If it feels like you're not, it's because the goals and standards you set for yourself are always a little higher than they were the month before. A work diary and good records are key to showing yourself that this is true. If every so often you review what you found challenging before, and realize that it's now total cake, you'll have an easier time handling new challenges. I used to hate quoting prices for my work, and frequently lowered them well before I had to. Flubbing a price negotiation is a quick way to lose a potential customer, and I was afraid to risk losing any business at all, even at the cost of working for less money than I needed. Now other details sometimes cause me difficulty, but I have no problem asking a client for, and getting, what I'm worth.

Take a Deep Breath and Think Big Picture

I let most of my clients know that I work out of my apartment. It explains why I meet them at their place of work and shows me to be a frugal and careful businessman.

Of course, it also lets them know that if they call my office at 11:30 at night, there's a good chance I'll be there to answer the phone. And a number of times I've gotten a major emergency dumped in my lap just when I was ready to knock off another chapter of a book I was reading, or, worse still, catch up on some projects for other clients.

Entrepreneurship lends itself to crisis-management thinking. A customer hands you a problem, and you do everything you can to deal with it quickly and efficiently. That's fine most of the time: the client will be satisfied, and you'll have one more good service call or product delivery under your belt.

But it also makes every problem a crisis, and it calls into use all of your biological crisis mechanisms that sent our ancestors up trees when the local fauna tried to turn them into dinner. That's wearying even when things go well, and it's a sure thing that every once in a while you'll get handed a problem that you *won't* be able to knock off quickly and simply. A festering problem is bad enough, but a crisis gone downhill is a good way to blow major circuits in your brain. ("This is your brain. This is your brain in crisis. . . .")

When you're in the middle of one of these situations, your first job is to distance yourself—mentally if that's good enough, physically if necessary—from the customer with the problem and any staff who might be aiding in your misery. If you are making things worse with internal negative thinking, tell yourself to shut up. Then sit down, take a deep breath, and remind yourself that, in all likelihood, the worst-case scenario of this outcome is not that bad. Usually the worst thing that a blown crisis can cause is a lost customer. You don't have the luxury of doing this often, but once in a while it's going to happen.

Envisioning the worst-case scenario is a great way of knocking some of the stress out of a problem. There are very few times when a single problem gone out of control can actually shut down your business or adversely affect your life in a way that you'll notice six months from now. But the "worst that can happen" can be pretty awful, which can give you the impetus to do what you need to get things right again. Focus adrenaline and stress into energy, but don't let the problem seem, or even become, bigger than it should be.

Handling Whole-Enchilada Days

Then again, sometimes a crisis can actually be pretty damn big. When the client with the problem represents 80 percent of your cash flow, or the lawyer tells you that a lawsuit is on the way unless you totally retool your plans, you might not be able to shrug things off as easily.

It might not be reassuring at these times, but keep in mind that every entrepreneur comes up against a major obstacle at some point, sometimes more than once. Every so often, the actions you take will determine the next six months or six years of your life and your business, and there's nothing you can do but take a deep breath and deal with it. Your first day on the job as your own boss is one of these times, and if you're lucky, once you're past that the worst will be over. The other 95 percent of us will have to learn to lay it all on the line and not become blithering idiots.

The first trick is to remember that even if the business is in a make-or-break situation, the business is not you. Debtors' prisons are out of style, and failed business owners are no longer drawn and quartered in most of the United States, although you might have to remind the judges of that. Even if you blow the entire business on a major deal that goes sour and your financial life goes down the drain, that doesn't take you with it. Many entrepreneurs sitting on millions of bucks have failed businesses in their backgrounds. That's one of the key advantages of being young: you can screw up really big and still have forty or fifty years to set things right.

None of this is going to make it easier to handle a major life-changing risk, which is exactly as it should be. Laying it all on the line should be extremely difficult, very rare, and ideally promise a major payoff in return for all the Pepto-

Bismol you'll be swilling in the meantime. And if that risk doesn't pay off, don't go looking for a high window, a bridge, or a strong rope. The failure of your business would be a major setback and a serious thing to consider, but it won't brand you a failure. It'll just make you feel like one for a little while, and then you'll use what you learned to get on with your next endeavor. Entrepreneurs (and, come to think of it, most human beings) never take those big risks because the fear of the big loss prevents them from ever trying. Don't let your fear prevent you from taking worthwhile risks—that's a surer path to stagnation and failure than anything else you could do.

How to Tell a Calculated Risk from a Wild-Ass Gamble

I'm nuts about gambling. Ever since I got my fake ID (no longer necessary, thank God), I've jaunted up to Atlantic City a few times a year, and I make an annual trip to Las Vegas for an intensive week of minor vices to get it out of my system.

When I was an undergrad, I was a pretty poor gambler. I knew what to do, but I had so little money that it was easy to lose everything I had. I must have been a serious glutton for punishment when I was younger, because my clearest memory of those trips is coming back in the car with only a few bucks in my pocket and a bank account that had been cleared out of the few twenties I had. Now I'm older, wiser, and wealthier, and a little smarter about how I spend my time in a casino.

My two favorite games are craps and blackjack. Craps is a dice game, and no matter how you slice it, it's serious gambling. There are roughly 10,000 bets you can play on the table. Some of them are pretty stupid and guarantee that the casino will take your money in short order. Others give a smaller edge to the "house." Regardless, it's a mathematical certainty that if you play long enough you will lose all your money. The only way to lower your risk is to do tricky things with the dice, and that *will* get you drawn and quartered.

Blackjack, on the other hand, is gambling for most people but can also be played as a game of calculated risk. Blackjack is a card game, and as it turns out the edge the casino has on you is dependent on what cards have been played. There are rare times when the player actually has a mathematical edge on the casino, and a good player can read the cards and act on that. Of course, many people play blackjack overestimating how much they know, and walk away totally battered by the cards.

I can sit down at a card table and tell you with reasonable accuracy how good the odds are for or against the casino. I can also tell you what the odds dictate to be the right thing to do at any given time. I've learned the hard way never to give this advice to strangers. After all, the whole point of gambling is that you aren't supposed to be able to predict what's going to happen next. Knowing the odds can't prevent a bad streak of cards, and even the best players (which I'm not) frequently get burned.

But in the long run, blackjack is a better game than craps. My actions affect the outcome in blackjack, and I can use my experience to better my odds. At the craps table, I'm just another schmo hoping for a lucky streak.

Gamblers like to use gaming as a metaphor for everything, so here's what I've learned about risk-taking in business from my contributions over the years to Donald Trump and friends:

Gambling Is Beyond the Control of the Gambler. If the risk you're taking is dependent on many things outside your control going the right way, you're gambling. If you have some control over the factors involved and know what steps you can take to move things in your favor, you're taking a calculated risk.

Stakes Should Be Low. I'm not any better at craps now than I was five years ago, but I'm a winner much more often. Back then a single roll could bankrupt my gambling stake; these days I can weather out a few bad shots and still stay in until things go right. A calculated risk uses a small portion of your resources, and can be taken frequently. The larger the stakes get in proportion to what you've got—in terms of time, money, or resources—the closer it gets to gambling.

Churning Will Burn You. Churning is taking your winnings and plowing them right back into another gamble. Profits from risky ventures should go into surer prospects. Plowing your money from a small-time gamble into consistently bigger schemes will break you.

Know the Odds or Don't Play the Game. The worst blackjack players are the ones who have read just enough to be dangerous. They confidently rely on skills they don't have, and end up wagering their rent when they should be miles from the tables. The less you can quantify the chances of a particular risk going your way, and the less knowledge you have of how to improve those odds, the more you're gambling.

Some Folks Have No Business Gambling. There are plenty of people who are addicted to gambling for its own sake; the thrill isn't the game or the win but the siren call of the risk itself. For these people, small losses turn into big losses as they vainly attempt to get back to even, while small wins turn into big losses as they foolishly hope for a better score. I know I've got a touch of this, and when I feel the fever hitting, I get far away from the gaming tables. Unrecognized, it can do you some major damage. Entrepreneurs have a great deal of control over their lives. If some part of themselves goes out of control in the quest for an adrenaline high, they can seriously screw up not only their businesses, but their lives.

The psychological profiles of an entrepreneur and a problem gambler are sometimes eerily similar. If anything in your history indicates you're a problem gambler or unable to accurately assess risks, then be that much more careful whenever you embark on anything less than a sure thing. If you've got this problem bad enough, you've got no business being an entrepreneur. Get a safer job until you can understand yourself well enough not to lose control.

T he germ of the idea for this discussion of risk management was a few words in Jim Schell's *The Brass Tacks Entrepreneur* (Henry Holt, 1993). Schell covers a lot of ground on risk-taking and the entrepreneurial psyche. I take this one off my shelf for a reread every six months.

Internet

Why You Need to Be On the Internet

An excellent discussion about risk-taking and the mechanics of risk management can be found online in Risks Digest, in the USENET group comp.risks. And slightly off-topic, most of what I know about gambling I learned from the USENET group rec.gambling. The participants there combine a love of the game with a serious interest in reducing risk and in applying mathematical rigor and major computer firepower to it. All of this is leavened with a healthy dose of philosophy about having fun while expending mental effort. If you have even a slight interest in gaming, I recommend spending some time here.

CHAPTER 15

The Big Question: Are You Successful Yet?

*T*his past year has been, by all standards, incredible for me. My income has doubled since last year, and all indications are that it will double again next year. My business is branching out into new areas that will be more profitable than my older, less-defined ideas. I am developing a nationwide team of consultants to sell services and expand my business, and everyone I've landed so far gives every indication of being a real superstar. And I've found the Holy Grail of consulting: publishing a book, which adds luster to my professional reputation and additional income to my bottom line.

My personal life has also been fairly spectacular. With the exception of several notable major setbacks, which were beyond the control of mere mortals, my quality of life is at the highest it's ever been. I'm involved in the best romantic relationship I've ever had, and we've moved to a new apartment that's triple the size of my old one. I have gadgets and gizmos aplenty, I travel more often than just about anyone I know, and I live in a part of Washington that can fairly be described as yuppie Disneyland.

Sounds good, huh? I'm not at the jet-helicopter stage, but by all accounts I'm still reaping the benefits and freedoms of successful entrepreneurial life.

And yet . . . I'll be the first person to tell you that I do not feel successful. The glow from my major miracles fades awfully quickly, and I barely get a bump from minor victories. On the flip side, the negatives in my life do an extremely good job of pulling me down.

After three years, I've come very close to serious entrepreneurial burnout. The first was a year ago, when I was hospitalized for physical exhaustion. The second was during the completion of this book, when mounting deadlines from my publisher and my clients and a personal tragedy put me out of commission for two weeks.

Too many other books portray the author as a god among businessmen, and the entrepreneurial battle as all wine and roses. Sure, they also talk about the risks and downsides, but not as much as the amazing victory stories and tales of the rewards at the end of the trail.

I am nowhere near the end of my trail; after three years in business, many people would still see me as a neophyte entrepreneur. I still have a lot to learn. Writing this book has, in many ways, been a cathartic experience for me, as I looked over the last three years of my life and saw the things that needed changing.

Like many others, I was too stupid to follow much of the advice given in the books I read, including some of what I've said here. Reading is not the same as doing and experiencing. My first task when I'm done writing the last words will be to sit down, reread my book, and be sure I've followed my own advice.

I suspect that there isn't much difference between you and me, at least in fundamental ways. Both of us are ambitious, stifled by other people's directives, and have an itch to build something on our own terms. Both of us are headfirst, damn-the-torpedoes types. And we both want to capitalize on the skills and talents that set us apart from the masses.

When you follow the road that I've taken for three years, it's natural you will hit some of the same obstacles that I have. There will be times that require miracle-working when your personal energy is so low it's a chore just to keep breathing.

Remember always that others have been where you are, and others will follow. These times are not so much a test of entrepreneurial ability as they are a test of self. If you have what it takes, then nothing can crush you. Even major defeats can be turned around, given time. At your core must lie an indomitable spirit, or you wouldn't have tried this in the first place. It was partially for these reasons that I chose to become an entrepreneur in the first place, as the fastest method of teaching myself the skills I'll need to reach my grandiose life plans—or the fastest way to learn that I don't have what it takes.

Three years in, I know three things to be true. The road so far has been dangerous and exhilarating. The future will have ups and downs even steeper than those I've hit before. And each survived disaster and brilliant success will lead me forward to the day when I am truly proud of myself, when I can bask in my accomplishments, and call myself an unqualified success. That battle can only be won on the inside.

Godspeed us both toward that day.

CHAPTER 16

Read This
in One Year

*F*irst of all, congratulations, and happy anniversary! It's a fair bet that you haven't yet given yourself credit for surviving the first year. Take a break, crack open a brew or a bottle of wine, and give yourself a pat on the back.

Now that you're comfortable, let me suggest some hard questions for you. A year ago when you first read this book and started a business, you probably had very little idea of what you were in for. No matter how many times someone tells you what's in your future, there's no substitute for experience. Chances are you've been weighed down more than once by that frozen twenty-pound chicken in your stomach, which I asked you to envision in chapter 2 as part of failure and fear, and you've probably also had a few euphoric highs to balance out those lows.

This is as good a time as any to decide whether or not it's worth it. Let's face it, entrepreneurship is simply not for everybody. Many people leap into it headfirst only to find the waters not to their liking. Unfortunately, it's much harder to shut down a business and look for a job than it is to just get fired. How do you explain to friends and family that you went and fired *yourself*?

Over the past year, you've probably had a few hard moments when you looked at yourself and found either the gumption to make it through, or the realization that you can't handle the pressure. Maybe you didn't tell anyone about this, but face it, you know where you stand. This is your life we're talking about. Staying on as your own boss when it's not what you want would be far worse than any job you could ever have. Closing down a business for your own personal well-being is not failure. It's an intelligent response to the pressures in your life and your search for bliss, the same attitudes that led you into the business in the first place.

What about the flip side? You've got what it takes to be in charge, but the day-to-day work just isn't what you want to do. You've found yourself—God forbid—*bored* by being the boss. Parts of it are fun, but the routine of your daily work has dragged you down far more quickly than you dreamt it would.

Some of this is unavoidable, and some of it is your own fault. Face it: even Abraham Lincoln had to shave every day and take trips to the loo. We read about the Bill Gateses of the world jetting about in first class and the Marc Andressens (of Netscape fame) becoming multibillionaires fresh of out of college, and we expect that our lives should be as filled with glory. Or at least, I do—this is a problem that I've been dealing with. The point is, all lives are filled with the heights of glory and the pits of despair, and all the space in the middle gets filled up with the mundane mush that makes up our daily schedules. No one is immune from this—no presidents, no power brokers, and no entrepreneurs.

The trick is to make the mush as life-fulfilling as possible. Life is what happens to us when we're making other plans— so be ready to take on the day-to-day drudgery and make the most of it.

On the other hand, if your business isn't giving you the peaks and troughs you desire, you might have to do some re-engineering of your work. I'm on what I think is my fourth career in the three years since I started the business—and I'll expand into a fifth when I get bored with what I'm doing now. You can change your business design for financial reasons or business reasons, but the most important reasons are probably personal: do at all times what you want to do. (Just delegate profitable work to someone else rather than shutting it down.)

Entrepreneurship is entirely what you make it. Your goals, dreams, and plans are going to change on a regular basis, as you learn more about your skills and desires. This would be a good time to go through this book again and write a fresh set of ideas for where to go next.

Entrepreneurship has been the most exasperating, frustrating, and terrifying experience I've ever subjected myself to. I wouldn't trade it for the world.

Online
Resources

*O*n the Web site for this book, I will be creating a one-stop shopping list of all the best entrepreneurial resources on the Internet. You can find it at

http://getnet. com/~creative.

This will be a joint effort between me, my readers, and interested Net citizens, so drop me a line with any resources you've found that you can't live without.

You can also sign up to be on an electronic mailing list for the discussion of ideas and questions generated by this book. Join it by writing to creative@getnet.com. That's also the place to reach me with your comments about this book. I'd love to hear them!

Web Sites

Fedworld is the wide world of government information on-line. If Uncle Sam has it on disk and wants you to see it, it's here. http://www.fedworld.com/

Yahoo is the best index of what you can find anywhere on the Internet. Browse here to your heart's delight. http://www.yahoo.com/

USENET Lists

biz hierarchy: This is a whole section of the USENET devoted to business. I've never found anything particularly useful here, but it's worth checking out for discussions that are germane to your work.

clari hierarchy: This special section of the USENET runs news feeds through hundreds of newsgroups. Your Internet provider has to pay extra for these, so many people don't get it. The clari business groups provide a lot of industry news that you won't find in the newspapers.

misc.entrepreneurs: The first USENET discussion for entrepreneurs, this is now flooded with useless marketing pitches for MLMs.

misc.entrepreneurs.moderated: This is the discussion that misc.entrepreneurs once was; it's much more worthwhile.

misc.business.consulting: This news group is dedicated to consulting in its various flavors.

Print
Resources

*I*n case it isn't absolutely clear yet, I've read a lot of books. Here are the ones I recommend for your total-immersion program:

Clark, Scott A. *Beating the Odds* (Amacom, 1991). A standard how-to-start-a-business book, but one of the better of the breed.

Covey, Stephen. *The Seven Habits of Highly Effective People* (Simon and Schuster, 1989). Covey can be blamed for unleashing a tide of self-help books from people who are not nearly as talented as he is. His seven habits are easy to digest and self-evidently true: "Seek first to understand, then to be understood." But it can be extremely hard to put the seven habits into practice; living up to the standards here can sometimes feel impossible. Worth reading every two years as a reminder to keep the big picture in perspective.

Covey, Stephen, with Roger and Judy Merrill. *First Things First* (Simon and Schuster, 1994). An expansion of the time-control system that Covey brings up in *Seven Habits*. Like the other book, it's hard to live up to, but you know he's right.

Goldstein, Arnold S. *Starting on a Shoestring* (John Wiley, 1984). An excellent list of ideas for starting a traditional big small business—that is, one requiring loans and financing. I'm not convinced by Goldstein's arguments for living with a heavy debt load. It seems like a ticket for major stress—but if your business idea requires financing that you don't have, this book will tell you how to land it.

Levinson, Jay Conrad. *Guerrilla Marketing* (Houghton Mifflin, 1993), *Guerrilla Marketing Attack* (Houghton Mifflin, 1989), and *Guerrilla Marketing Excellence* (Houghton Mifflin, 1993). If you want to become a millionaire, here's how to do it. Utterly brilliant. Put these books on your shelves and devour them as thoroughly as possible.

Mackay, Harvey. *Swim with the Sharks without Being Eaten Alive* (Morrow, 1988), *Beware the Naked Man Who Offers You His Shirt* (Morrow, 1990), and *Sharkproof* (Harper-Business, 1993). Mackay and Jim Schell, listed below, are two men I really want to meet. Mackay's the head of Mackay Envelopes, and has dozens of brilliant insights into business. His books are a little slanted toward the corporate lifestyle rather than the small business, and *Sharkproof* is more applicable to job seekers than job creators, but all three are well worth reading.

RoAne, Susan. *How to Work a Room* (Shapoksky Publishers, 1988). I found most of the tips here to be self-evident, but then again I was born to schmooze. For the less self-confident and aggressive among you, this will give you a lot of great tips for networking.

Robbins, Tony. *Awaken the Giant Within* (Simon and Schuster, 1992) and *Unlimited Power* (Simon and Schuster, 1986). The king of the propeller heads. Robbins would have you believe that in fifteen minutes you can reprogram yourself to become a god amongst men, get rid of all your bad habits, and live a life of bursting vitality and vigor. The hell of it is, it seems to be true. It's all based on a technique called Neuro-Linguistic Programming, which has some amazing effects. But I've never been able to get it to work from the books, and Robbins hasn't convinced me with his infomercials to buy the $195 audiotape series. Still a fascinating read.

Schell, Jim. *The Brass Tacks Entrepreneur* (Henry Holt, 1993) and *Small Business Management Guide* (Henry Holt, 1994). Schell is totally shameless in letting us know about his victories and failures—and we're the better for it. I recognized in him a kindred soul, and gained a lot of strength from the stories he told of making it through on his own. His books are not only informative, but inspirational.

Zinsser, William. *On Writing Well* (Harper Perennial, 1994). I read this book twice while I was writing this one. Any mistakes found herein are not Zinsser's fault. His essays provide an excellent stroll through the finer points of grammar and structure, with an excellent discussion on the use of different writing styles for various purposes. A great book for those just jumping into business writing and for those who need a refresher course.

Small Business Administration Resources

*D*on't forget your Uncle Sam when you're looking for good business advice—and even a few freebies like professional tips from retired entrepreneurs, computer shareware you can use to plan your business, and more. The U.S. Small Business Administration has field offices in just about every major city (and many not-so-major ones). Check the government section ("Blue Pages") of your phone directory for the SBA office near you. Or better yet, check out the SBA's site on the World Wide Web at: http://www.sbaonline.sba.gov. A wealth of information is available, and you'll also find some of that helpful software. Here are a few of the SBA's programs that could prove useful to you:

Service Corps of Retired Executives (SCORE). Has more than 13,000 volunteers who conduct training and one-on-one counseling at no charge.

Small Business Development Centers. These offer training, counseling, research, and other services at more than 600 locations.

Developing Your Business Plan Workshop. This online manual is loaded with advice for start-up businesses, including information on marketing, writing business plans, competition, choosing a location, pricing and sales strategies, management issues, and more. It's located at the SBA's World Wide Web site (address above).

Workers of the World, Eat Pasta!

*I*t should be pretty clear from my asides in this book where my politics lie. I'm a member of what sometimes appears to be a dying breed: a liberal in Washington.

But no matter what your politics are, I heartily recommend that you devote a percentage of your entrepreneurial time and energy to some cause of your choosing, even if that cause is diametrically opposed to the causes I espouse. Activism is its own reward and its own virtue. I am convinced that two active fighters on opposite sites of the same cause will do more to ultimately fix the world's problems than any number of couch potatoes who just complain about those problems.

Members of our generation have absolutely no excuse for not getting involved. It's our world, and we'll have to live in it for decades. Out of pure self-interest, you should find motivation to make it a better one.

Shortly after I moved to D.C., I was lucky enough to participate in a conference in New York City that simulated the activities of the United Nations. I met some amazing people there, and over the course of our meeting, we all noticed that a large number of us worked with nonprofit organizations devoted to liberal causes in Washington, D.C. Ironically, if we hadn't all traveled to New York, we never would have found out about each other's existence. Many of us were working on similar projects, sometimes even the same projects—and all of that effort would have been needlessly duplicated if we had never been able to compare notes and combine our resources. Given that liberal nonprofit budgets can generously be called minuscule, this seemed ridiculous from a financial standpoint, and a waste of our time from any point of view.

On the train back home, three of us founded an informal organization to ameliorate this problem. We eventually christened it the Noodle Club and began holding biweekly dinner meetings for dedicated young activists working for liberal causes. The noodle name came from the fact that our meetings are usually held in restaurants where the food is affordable even for people on no income—and that usually means pasta.

Noodle Club meetings are informal and friendly. The entire dinner time is spent socializing and relaxing. Following dinner, we have a period of introductions and what we call "Shameless Self-Promotion," an opportunity for anyone to announce the work their organization is doing, any job openings, or any personal issues—such as a job search or something else—for which the club member wants some help. Dues are voluntary and low-priced, and attendance is open to anyone.

We had no idea what we were doing when we started Noodle Club, but it's been a significant source of contacts for all of us. Noodle Club hasn't generated much business for me over the years—the organizations that are drawn to it frequently can only hire me at a very reduced rate—but it's one of the most important things on my schedule, and I contribute a significant amount of time to running it. This has been one of the best perks of being self-employed: the ability to dedicate my time and energy to important causes of my choosing. In my value system, there would be little point to devoting myself to building a business that gave me the freedom to set my own agenda, if that agenda were solely devoted to personal gain.

Noodle Club has branches in Washington and New York, and we're looking to open chapters in other cities around the country. If you're interested, send an e-mail message to NoodleClub@aol.com.

A

"Abyss," planning against the, 17
accessories, 141–142
advisory board, *see* board of advisors
Amway, 51, 53
Aniston, Jennifer, 2
arrogance, 199–201

B

balance, sense of, 238
barriers to entry, 105–106
barter, 178–181
benefits of products and services, 187

billable time, 71–73
billing by hour vs. by project, 74–76
blood donations for money, 175–176
board of advisors, 220
body language, 203–204
brainstorming, 32
Buchanan, Joey, 22–23
Bugs Bunny, 50
business cards, 157–159, 205–206
business failures, 20–21
business incubators, 135
business permits, 165